"In the deserts of our modern cities,
many perish in the noontime heat
of daily life. The anxieties of life
—making a living, tensions of the office,
the pressures of home and the difficulty
of family life in a modern world
wither the soul and bring many to the end
of themselves.
"At the same time, in the same city deserts,
others smile and float through their problems
on a river of serenity
that causes onlookers to be utterly amazed."
What makes the difference in merely existing
or really living? In the pages that follow,
you'll find the answers that will have you
saying with Dr. D. James Kennedy,
THIS IS THE LIFE!

This is the Life!

Guidelines for Christian Growth
by Dr. D. James Kennedy

Discussion Questions and Study Helps
by the Rev. James C. Bland
Minister of Follow-up
Coral Ridge Presbyterian Church

A Division of G/L Publications
Glendale, California, U.S.A.

Published by
Regal Books Division, G/L Publications
Glendale, California 91209, U.S.A.

Library of Congress Catalog No. 72-97646
ISBN 0-8307-0206-7

Scripture quoted from *The Authorized Version* (KJV)

The publishers do not necessarily endorse the entire contents
of all publications referred to in this book.

Contents

Introduction

A teaching and discussion guide for individual or group study with THIS IS THE LIFE! is available in a G/L Learning Pac from your local church supplier. A 3-cassette album of THIS IS THE LIFE! is also available.

Contents

Introduction

Introduction

Happy Birthday, friend!

Whether it was just today, yesterday, a year ago or even ten years ago, the day you received Jesus Christ into your heart and life as Saviour and Lord was your birthday. On that day you were born spiritually into the family of God, and whenever it was or whenever the anniversary of that day is, I say "happy birthday" to you.

On your day of decision, you no doubt heard no angelic voices or saw any heavenly visions, yet still for you it was the day when all things began to become new. It is a date to record, to remember and to celebrate, for your spiritual birthday is even more important than your physical birthday.

Why?

Because as Jesus Christ said in John 3:3, "Verily, verily, I say unto thee, Except a man be born again, he cannot see the kingdom of God."

And now, having been born again—born spiritually, you need to grow spiritually. You may very well be saying to yourself, "Yes, you're right, but what do I do now? Where do I go from here?"

This brings us to the matter of spiritual diet. In 1 Peter 2:2 we are told, "As newborn babes, desire the sincere milk of the word, that ye may grow thereby: if so be ye have tasted that the Lord is gracious."

". . . That ye may grow thereby." Spiritually, as well as physically, good food and proper diet are essential for strong, rapid growth to full maturity. It is my desire—and I know it is yours—for you to grow into full Christian maturity. That is why I have written this book—to help you grow as a Christian. Its purpose is to provide you with the essential basic nutrients of a full, balanced spiritual diet necessary for you as a growing Christian.

So *This Is the Life!* is written with you in mind, to provide you with some guidelines for growing strong and tall in the Christian life. It is prayerfully intended to guide you into THE LIFE found only in Him.

Yours in Christ

D. James Kennedy

P.S. To help you get the most benefit from this series of studies, permit me to offer a few suggestions. As you read along in this book you will find consecutively numberered questions interspersed into the text at strategic points. Don't skip over these questions. They are important to you, and Rev. James C. Bland, our Minister of Follow-up, put them there for a purpose: to cause you to stop and think about the material you have read in relation to yourself. By answering each question as you read along, you can check out your understanding of what you have read before going any further.

If you are reading this book and simultaneously listening to my companion tapes (from which this text is taken), simply stop your cassette player at each numbered question in the text and answer that question. After you have answered the question satisfactorily, turn your player back on and listen to the tape again, following along in the book until you come to the next question, and so on, to the end of a chapter. I recommend that you do not attempt more than one chapter a day.

The book and tapes for *This Is the Life!* may be studied individually or in small groups. For small group study, simply follow the procedure outlined above.

For more in-depth study, Rev. Bland has provided further helps at the end of each chapter. Do take time to study the suggested Scriptures and their context, examine the appropriate question from the Westminster Confession of Faith, and also do the recommended readings.

May God bless and reward you richly as you undertake this study of guidelines for Christian growth.

CHAPTER 1

Knowing You Are Going to Heaven

You have made the most important decision anyone can make in life. You have decided to receive Jesus Christ as your own Saviour and Lord. You have begun a new adventure, a great adventure, walking with Him.

But there are many things you now need to know and learn. One of the first things is to be absolutely sure of your destination; to know for certain that you are going to heaven.

1. What is one of the most important truths to be sure of in your new relationship to Jesus Christ?

The Scripture says in 1 John 5:13, "These things have I written unto you that believe on the name of the Son of God; that ye may know that ye have eternal life. . . ."

Isn't that a tremendous proclamation?

2. Look up this important truth in your Bible. Then mark 1 John 5:13 by underlining it. Now commit it to memory.

1

Even the most casual perusal of the New Testament will reveal that one of the most striking characteristics of the apostles and the entire Apostolic Church was the element of certainty.

These were men who *knew*. They didn't hope, they didn't wish, they didn't merely think—they knew! They knew their sins were forgiven; and they knew they had received eternal life. They knew beyond all doubt that they were on their way to heaven.

3. What was one of the most striking characteristics of the Apostolic Church? What did they "know"?

Today, many find this to be the most startling fact on the pages of the New Testament. And yet we read that they said, "We know that we have passed from death unto life" (1 John 3:14). "We know that we are of God" (1 John 5:19). We know "in whom we have . . . the forgiveness of sins" (Ephesians 1:7).

"We know that, when he shall appear, we shall be like him" (1 John 3:2). We know that "to be absent from the body" is "to be present with the Lord" (2 Corinthians 5:8). We know that nothing can "separate us from the love of God, which is in Christ Jesus our Lord" (Romans 8:39).

We know that we know! Affirmation piled on top of affirmation. They not only knew, but they knew that they knew!

It was this certainty, this confidence, this unshakable faith that enabled the apostles to withstand every difficulty, to overcome every obstacle, and to turn the world right side up for Jesus Christ. This was no mere vain boast but a ringing, glorious affirmation of faith in Jesus Christ; a stirring testimony to the risen Lord Jesus.

4. What was the result of the "knowing"?

Perhaps nowhere in the world is the contrast between the modern church and the Apostolic Church more glaringly seen than in this area of certainty. You may visit church after church today. As you do, study the faces of the people as they come in and go out, ask them questions, inquire of their beliefs, examine their lives, and you will find that this element of certainty is conspicuously absent. Certainty of faith is hard to find today.

5. What element is conspicuously absent from the modern-day church member?

In the nineteenth century, Thomas Huxley coined a word which describes this attitude, this lack of certainty, this not knowing. The word is *agnostic*. Agnostic comes from two Greek words, *nosis* (to know) and the alpha primitive *a* (to take away what you know).

This is also a biblical word, and Paul used it frequently. However, it's not translated into English as "agnostic"; it's translated somewhat differently. Listen to what Paul says: "Brethren, I would not have you ignorant" (1 Corinthians 12:1). The Greek

3

word here is "agnostic" (the Latin form is "ignoramus") which means "not to know."

So Paul says he would not have us not to know. Not to know about what? Not to know about God, and not to know about eternal life.

Is this not a perfect description of many church members everywhere today? They think, they wish, they surmise, they theorize, they philosophize, and they hope they are going to heaven. But when the end comes, they cross their fingers, close their eyes and die without any certainty of heaven.

How utterly at variance this is with the ringing affirmations of the New Testament church. How sad it is that when most people today sing "Blessed Assurance," it is little more than a mockery, for few of them know anything of that "Blessed assurance, Jesus is mine. Oh, what a foretaste of glory divine."

What are the results of this lack of certainty in the Church today?

6. *What do you think will be the results of this lack of certainty in the modern-day church member?*

The results can be seen everywhere. When certitude is gone, people no longer know what will happen to them when they die. When they lack certainty, when their ringing assurance is gone, then gone also will be their joy.

Gone will be the smiling faces. Gone will be the bold witness for Christ. Gone also will be faithful service to Jesus Christ, because all the blessings of the Christian life flow from the wellspring or the assurance of eternal life. They are the result of it, even as the river flows from the spring.

A little girl came home from school one day and said, "Mommy, I've learned how to punctuate."

Thinking this to be quite an accomplishment for a girl of her age, her mother said, "Well, that's fine, sweetie. Tell me, how do you punctuate?"

The little girl said, "If something is definitely certain, you put a hatpin after it. But if it's not really certain, or you're not sure about it, then you just put a buttonhook after it."

Hatpins and buttonhooks! I think we might divide all the church members everywhere into these two categories: hatpins and buttonhooks.

Which one are you?

If you're not a hatpin, maybe you never got the point! For you, life and death and eternity are still one huge black question mark. You just don't know. But you can know.

Would you like to know?

You can know most assuredly. You can know for certain that you are going to heaven. You can say with the apostle Paul, "We are confident, I say, and willing rather to be absent from the body, and to be present with the Lord" (2 Corinthians 5:8).

Would you like to be able to say that and mean it? There are many who can. I hope you will join them, perhaps today.

Only recently I attended a meeting of the Federation of Churches in New Orleans. As I walked through the Sunday School wing of the Presbyterian Church where the meeting was held, I

5

glanced into the kitchen and saw a large hulk of a man, a black man, doing something in there.

I walked on out of the Sunday School wing into the yard, but something seemed to grasp me, stop me dead, and pull me back. Back in the wing again, I looked into the kitchen and saw that this man was washing the dishes.

Feeling God was leading me to say something, I said, "Good morning. How are you?"

"Fine," he said.

I introduced myself and asked his name. His name was Harvey.

For some reason I suddenly felt compelled to say to him, "You know, Harvey, we're in town on a spiritual mission for all of the churches here in New Orleans, and we're talking about spiritual truths. You've probably been working around the church for some time. I'd like to ask you a question."

He said, "Go ahead."

So I continued. "Have you come to a place in your life where you know for certain that if you die tonight you would go to heaven?"

This huge man fixed his jaw, set his face very seriously, looked down at the floor for a long silent moment, and said, "No, no, I don't know that."

I asked, "Are you aware that it is possible to know?"

"Yes," he said. "I know that. You see, I'm a minister in a local church. I work here in the daytime, but I've been a minister there for fourteen years."

Then I knew why God brought me back. I asked him on what he was basing his hope of eternal life. You know what it was? It was the same old answer: his own efforts to try to do good, to try to live a good life, to try to keep the Ten Commandments, to try to follow the Golden Rule.

Even though Harvey was a minister in a church, he had never grasped the gospel of Christ. I had the thrill of standing right there in the kitchen and telling him of the glorious good news of Jesus Christ, that God is willing to freely give us eternal life simply by trust in Christ.

We then stepped into the next room and sat down. I asked him, "Harvey, would you like to receive the gift of eternal life right now? Would you like to cease trusting in yourself and start trusting in Christ who died for your sins on the cross?"

"Oh yes!" he said. "I really would! I really would."

"All right," I said, "let's do it right now."

We prayed, and it was the most glorious thing to see this man's face just glow with joy.

"Harvey," I said, "if you were to die tonight, where would you go?"

"Praise the Lord," he said, "I'd go right to heaven!"

Why that's enough to make even a Presbyterian say "Hallelujah!"

I came back to the church the next day, and the first thing I did was go to the Sunday School wing and find the kitchen to see my new friend. There he was eating lunch—a sandwich in one hand and the Gospel of John in the other.

"Harvey," I said, "how are you?"

"I'm great," he said. "I was just wishing you would come in here. I preached in my church last

7

night, and we had a revival that lasted till eleven o'clock at night. When I got through, all the children ran up and threw their arms around me. Later, one old elder said to me, 'Those were the most wholesome words I've ever heard in our church.'"

Isn't it wonderful to see the glory of God in the face of a man who has come to experience the grace of God? Grace is simply glory in the bud, and glory is grace come to full bloom.

Already a pipeline to God had been set up, and He poured a little bit of heaven into that man's soul. Harvey was no longer a buttonhook; he was now a very happy hatpin. Now he can sing "Blessed assurance, Jesus is mine" and really mean it.

7. According to the story of Harvey, the black minister, what must be understood and believed before a person can be certain of going to heaven?

The sad thing is that there are millions of people today who don't know for sure they have eternal life. And they are so far from the truth of the Scripture, they don't even know it's possible to have this knowledge.

A young lady, teeming with doubts, once said she was certain no one could be certain. We trust that when she grows a little older and wiser, she will know better.

Shall we take the position that it is impossible for the Almighty God who has created the universe— who has formed our mouths, ears and minds—to make Himself known to us? Shall we take this position in light of all the contrary evidence of the Scripture and the history of the Church?

The Bible says firmly, "These (things) are written, that ye might believe" (John 20:31), that you may know. Over and over again the emphasis is the same: that you may *know*, that you may *know*, that you may *know* that you have eternal life.

Go through the First Epistle of John—not the Gospel, but the epistle—and underline the word "know." You will be amazed at how often it appears and at what God might say to you through that exercise.

This certainty, this blessed and joyous assurance was not only one of the hallmarks of the Early Church; it was also one of the outstanding facts about the Reformation Church.

8. What was the hallmark of the Early Church and a fact of the Reformation Church?

During the Middle Ages, this assurance was lost. And the reason it was lost was because the Church had turned away from the truth of the Scripture. Men no longer rested on the merits and cross of Jesus Christ, but began to trust in their own goodness, their own efforts, their own piety, their own good works. And, at that point, they lost their assurance and their certainty.

9. Why was this certainty lost during the Middle Ages?

Then in 1517, Martin Luther nailed his 95 theses

to the church door at Wittenberg. But behind his nailing of those theses, there had come to Luther the unshakable certainty that God had received him just as he was. Luther *knew* that God had accepted him, justified him, forgiven him, and given him eternal life. All the Reformers—whether Luther, Calvin, Knox, Zwingli or Wesley—said, "We know that we have eternal life."

This knowledge is a part of each one of the great Reformed creeds of Protestantism. The Westminster Confession of Faith, the creed of the Presbyterians, has a whole chapter dedicated to this assurance of salvation. It says not only that we may be assured of salvation, but that we may have an infallible assurance of that salvation.

The Heidelberg Catechism—that personal catechism loved by millions in Europe and America, begins with the famous question, "What is your only comfort, in life and in death?" The answer in part is, "That I belong—body and soul, in life and in death—not to myself but to my faithful Saviour, Jesus Christ, who at the cost of His own blood has fully paid for all my sins and has completely freed me from the dominion of the devil. . . . Therefore, by His Holy Spirit, He also assures me of eternal life. . . ."

10. What is the famous first question asked by the Heidelberg Catechism? Carefully read the answer once again.

Remember the question which the Heidelberg

10

Catechism asks: "What is your only comfort, in life and in death?"

The assurance that you belong to Jesus Christ is the only comfort in life and death for anyone. There is no other. This certainty will dispel the clouds from your soul. It will enable you to go through any affliction or adversity. How blessed indeed is the assurance this certainty can give.

How dreary and dark and foreboding is life without the assurance of everlasting happiness. The sad thing is that modern liberalism—with all its denials of historic Christianity—has crept into the fold as a wolf in sheep's clothing, robbing millions of God's sheep of that blessed assurance which God desires them to have.

Because of this fact, in many churches today, not only is the gospel not proclaimed, it is denied outright. The result is that countless millions of people have grown up with the most erroneous concepts of Christianity. They have spiritual distortions at best, or arrant lies and falsehoods at worst. The main reason why people do not have this assurance is because they entertain completely false concepts of what Christianity is and what the Christian gospel says.

11. What is the main reason people do not have this assurance or knowledge that they are going to heaven?

You can believe the statements of the apostles, of the reformers, and of those others down through the centuries who have known that they have eternal

11

life. And you can believe me as I declare to you now, "I *know* I am going to heaven!"

I wonder if your reaction is, "That is braggadocio. That is a vain and boasting fellow. That is the utmost in conceit."

If that is your attitude, then you have completely missed the message of Christianity. You might as well have been reared in a pagan land, for there is no boasting whatsoever in my claim—not the least.

Why?

Because, you see, I *am* going to heaven. But it's not because of what I've done or because of what I am. It's because of what Christ has done for me. I'm going to heaven not because of what I am, but in spite of what I am.

Salvation is a free gift, and you can't boast about a gift. You can only be thankful. It is no achievement of mine. It is not because I think that I am good or pious or holy, because I know that I am none of these. I know I am sinful and wicked and I belong in hell. But I am going to heaven!

That is the gospel, the good news of Jesus Christ, that "God so loved the world, that he gave his only begotten Son, that whosoever believeth in him should not perish, but have everlasting life" (John 3:16).

"For by grace are ye saved through faith; and that not of yourselves: it is the gift of God: not of works, lest any man should boast" (Ephesians 2:8,9).

The passage that we began with (1 John 5:13) tells us that these things are written that "ye may know that ye have eternal life."

12

What things are written?

We read that God has declared that He has given to those who trust in His Son, eternal life. "God hath given to us eternal life, and this life is in his Son" (1 John 5:11).

Therefore, we take God at his word. It is merely a matter of not insulting God. The Scripture says that if we "believeth not the record that God gave of his Son" (1 John 5:10), we make God a liar.

12. Why must we take God at His word when He declares that "these things (are) written"?

It is blatant blasphemy to declare that God is a liar. But many people are doing it. Why? Because they say they believe in Jesus Christ, yet they also say they do not know that they are going to heaven.

Are you making God a liar? God says those who trust in His Son will be received into heaven, that they already have eternal life. This is an entirely new dimension of life which begins right now.

Have you trusted in His Son? Do you have eternal life? Are you taking God at His word? If so, you can rejoice in that assurance.

13. Are you taking God at His word? Summarize in one paragraph what it means for you to "take God at His word."

An old Scottish lady was dying and, as was the custom in those days, the minister came by to see if she really had true faith. As she lay dying on her bed, he said, "Do you still trust in Christ?"

"Ah, yes I do," she replied. "He is my only hope in life and in death."

Then the minister said, "Do you believe that He will take you to heaven?"

"Yes," she replied, "I know He will."

"But," he asked, "suppose that He doesn't?"

The old woman thought for a moment and replied, "Ah, God may do what He wills, but if He doesn't take me to heaven, He will lose more than I. Though I will lose my soul, God will lose His honor, for He has sworn that those who trust in His Son will never perish."

God has condescended to swear an oath in order that we might have the assurance we need.

Sir Michael Faraday, the great scientist, had come to the end of his distinguished career. Someone said to him on his deathbed, "Sir Michael, what speculations do you have now?"

He said, "Speculations! Man, I have none! I have certainties! I thank God that I don't rest my dying head upon speculations. 'For I know whom I have believed, and am persuaded that he is able to keep that which I have committed unto him against that day' " (2 Timothy 1:12).

It is simply a matter of trusting in the Word of God, of taking God at His promise.

A woman came to Dwight Moody one day and said, "Mr. Moody, I can't believe. I just can't believe!"

He asked, "Believe whom?"

"You don't understand. I just can't believe."

"Believe whom?" Moody asked again.

"No, you don't understand."

"I do understand," he answered. "You don't understand."

Do you believe God? God says, "He that hath the Son hath life (eternal)" (1 John 5:12) "and shall not come into condemnation" (John 5:24), and "shall never perish" (John 10:28). "He that believeth on the Son of God hath the witness in himself" (1 John 5:10).

Do you believe God? Do you take Him at His word? If we have trusted in Christ, then He has made us new creatures (2 Corinthians 5:17), and with the author of the Song of Solomon, we can say, "My beloved is mine, and I am his" (2:16). With Job we can declare, "I know that my redeemer liveth, and that he shall stand at the latter day upon the earth" (19:25), and I "shall see him" (1 John 3:2) face to face. We can sing with Fanny Crosby, the blind hymnist, "Blessed assurance, Jesus is mine."

Is that assurance yours? Are you a hatpin or a buttonhook? These things are written "that ye may *know* (italics added) that ye have eternal life" (1 John 5:13).

If you have not yet come to that place of blessed assurance, if you are not yet sure that you have eternal life, then right now would you tell the Lord Jesus Christ, in the silence of your own heart: "Lord Jesus, I do believe that you have died for me and paid for my sins. I do trust in you as my Saviour and Lord. And I believe your promise that right now I have everlasting life and shall never perish. I thank you for it. In Thy name. Amen."

As you begin this day with God, may I encourage you to spend a little time reading the Gospel of

John and talking to Christ in prayer just as though He were present with you—for that is exactly where He is.

"Blessed Lord Jesus Christ, I thank you that this dear one has come to place his trust in you, has accepted your promise and has received the gift of eternal life. I pray that, if there are still any doubts that linger, you will by your Spirit, even now, dispel those doubts and enable him to trust in your Word completely, for you can never lie. In Thy name. Amen."

Study Helps

1. Examine in context the following Bible passages on assurance: Ephesians 1:13,14; Hebrews 6:11,12,17,18; 2 Peter 1:4,5,10,11; 1 John 2:3,14,18, 19,21,24; 1 John 4:13,16; 1 John 5:13.

2. Study the *Westminster Confession of Faith,* Chapter 20: "Of the Assurance of Grace and Salvation," in *The Confession of Faith of The Presbyterian Church in the United States.* Richmond, Virginia: The Board of Christian Education, 1965.

3. Read the following books:

Graham, Billy. *Peace with God.* New York: Doubleday & Co., Inc., 1953. Note Chapter 12, "How to Be Sure."

Ryle, J.C. *Holiness.* Greenwood, South Carolina: Attic Press, 1952. Note Chapter 7, "Assurance."

Griffiths, Michael C. *Christian Assurance.* London: Inter-Varsity Press, 1962.

Brooks, Thomas. *Heaven on Earth.* Swengel, Pennsylvania: Reiner Publications, 1961.

Gerstner, John H. *Theology for Everyman*. Chicago: Moody Press, 1965. Note chapter on "Assurance: How We Know That We Know Christ."

CHAPTER 2

Staying Right with God

The first day of your new life with Jesus Christ is the greatest day of your life. It is the day in which you know that your sins are forgiven that you are on your way to an eternal heaven.

We have considered how to get right with God through trusting Christ. Now we want to consider how you can stay right with God day after day and year after year. Our text for this study is Colossians 2:6,7, where we read, "As ye have therefore received Christ Jesus the Lord, so walk ye in him: rooted and built up in him, and stablished in the faith, as ye have been taught, abounding therein with thanksgiving."

"Ye did run well; who did hinder you that ye should not obey the truth?" (Galatians 5:7). This is the question of the apostle Paul and is the question —no doubt—that many Christians ask themselves.

Why?

There are many who have begun the Christian life well. They have come to that day in their experience where they have heard the glad tidings of great joy. They have seen for the first time the glories of the gospel and the grace of God in Jesus Christ. They have received the free gift of eternal life. They have with raptured souls embraced by faith the Saviour as Lord and Master of their lives. They have walked forth from that moment into a new kingdom with a new joy and a new purpose.

But alas, in many cases, not long after beginning the Christian life, that joy is dissolved and that experience of the presence of God is no longer with them. That purpose in life seems thwarted. Even the assurance is diminished. They know not what to do for they really do not know what has happened to them.

The answer to what has happened is very simple. Sin has entered into their lives; it has hidden the face of God from them. It has robbed them of their joy and peace; it has taken away the awareness of God's presence. They feel themselves forsaken by God and many completely despair of going on with the Lord.

1. What has happened in many Christians' lives to take the joy, the peace, the purpose and even the assurance out of their daily walk with Jesus Christ?

We need to understand what God would have us do in this matter of sin in our lives as believers. Perhaps you are one who would say with King David,

"Restore unto me the joy of thy salvation" (Psalm 51:12).

Or, as one who would cry, "Oh, God, grant unto me again that first love as in the first blush of my love affair with Thee. Help me, for 'my soul is cast down within me'" (Psalm 42:6).

"As ye have therefore received Christ Jesus the Lord, so walk ye in him" (Colossians 2:6). Hide this verse in your heart. Write it upon the walls of your mind that you may read it often.

This is God's secret of walking in the Christian life; of not only getting right with God, but also of staying right with Him. Do you remember it? Say it again: "As ye have therefore received Christ Jesus the Lord, so walk ye in him."

2. What is the secret of staying right with God?

We do not become Christians by joining a church, nor by being baptized, nor by living a good life. We become Christians by receiving the living Person of Jesus Christ into our own hearts. Christ "came unto his own, and his own received him not. But as many as received him, to them gave he power to become the sons of God" (John 1:11,12).

This is how you become a Christian, and this is also how you are to live the Christian life. The whole sum and substance of Christianity is the reception of the Person of Jesus Christ. He *is* the Christian faith. He is its essence, its object, its source. He is "the way, the truth, and the life" (John 14:6).

How did we receive Christ? We received Christ as Saviour and Lord by repentance and faith.

3. How does one become a Christian? What does repentance mean to you? What does faith mean to you?

As Jesus began His ministry, He said, "The kingdom of God is at hand: repent ye, and believe the gospel" (Mark 1:15). These were His first words: "Repent and believe the gospel." So this is how you became a Christian. This is the way that you received the gift of eternal life—by repentance and faith.

Repentance is a determination of mind to turn from sin by the power that God will give us and to apprehend the mercy of God in Jesus Christ on the cross. When we see the odiousness of our own sin in the light of the cross, we come to despise it.

We are to repent and believe the gospel. The gospel means "glad tidings—good news." The good news is that Christ has come; that God, for Christ's sake, forgives us; that God, for Christ's sake, grants to us eternal life; that God, for Christ's sake, justifies us freely; that God, for Christ's sake, receives us into His family as His own dear children. This is what is meant by salvation by grace.

Some have asked, "How can salvation be by grace if we must repent?" God requires that we repent and believe in order that we may be saved. But God also freely gives us, by His own Holy Spirit, the gifts of repentance and faith. Faith is a gift from God, and so is repentance. The early

Christians in Jerusalem glorified God because He granted repentance unto the Gentiles. (See Acts 11:18.)

The Bible says, "The servant of the Lord must not strive; but be gentle . . . instructing those that oppose themselves; if God peradventure will give them repentance . . ." (2 Timothy 2:24,25).

What is needed for salvation is repentance and faith that we may be justified. What is given by God is repentance and faith. That which God requires, He also freely gives in order that the whole may be of grace. Salvation is of grace because salvation is entirely of God. This is how you became a Christian. And this is how you can live the Christian life.

4. Why is salvation or becoming a Christian entirely of grace?

We are justified by the grace of God. We are regenerated by the grace of God. We are sanctified by the grace of God. And we are ultimately glorified by the grace of God when the last vestiges of sin are removed as we enter into heaven. Thus we see that salvation from the beginning to the end is all of God and not of man. It is entirely His free grace.

Grace means totally unmerited favor; totally unearned and undeserved favor. We need to grasp this truth. We are not received by God because of some goodness in ourselves. We are not received by God because of what we are, but rather in spite of what we are.

We are received not because of our nature, but because of His nature. We are received by God not because of what we are, but because of what God is. He is the God of all grace. Salvation is of God. It is freely bestowed as a gift from Him. This also is the secret of the Christian life: "As ye have therefore received Christ Jesus the Lord, so walk ye in him" (Colossians 2:6). We are kept also by the grace of God.

The entire epistle to the Galatians is written to counteract one great heresy—that the Christian life begins by grace, but then proceeds by human works. Galatians says that salvation begins, continues and is completed by grace alone. We do not begin in the Spirit and then proceed in the flesh. As asks Paul the Apostle, "O foolish Galatians, who hath bewitched you, that ye should not obey the truth?" (Galatians 3:1).

Our life with God is entirely by His grace. The great perversion of Christianity which may creep in at the point of forgiveness, the point of justification or the point of sanctification, is simply that we must earn or that we *can* earn the favor of God by our goodness. God did not accept us because of any goodness in ourselves. And He does not keep us because of any such supposed goodness.

5. *What is the great perversion of Christianity? Why is it so easy to think this way?*

If you are a child of God—and I trust that in sincerity you have turned over your life to Christ—then you were chosen as such before the foundation

23

of the world. The Bible says that God has chosen us before the foundation of the world (Ephesians 1:4), that He sent His Son to die for us (Romans 8:32), and that He then sent His Holy Spirit to draw us unto Himself (Ephesians 2:18).

God knew from all eternity everything that you were and everything that you would be. When God redeemed you He knew what you would do today, what you would do tomorrow, and what you would do next week—and next year. He did not choose you because of any goodness that He saw in you. Therefore, He does not keep you because of any goodness in you.

Is this not also true with you and with me? You do not love your children because they are good, because they are clean, or because they are well-behaved or well-mannered or well-dressed. No, just the contrary. You do all in your power to make them well-behaved, well-dressed, well-mannered and clean, because you love them. You do not love them because they are bathed; you bathe them because you love them. This is the teaching of God's Word. And this is the teaching that can change your life if you will realize that just as you are, God —for Christ's sake—receives you.

Does this minimize sin? Not in the least, because sin was fully dealt with on the cross. There between heaven and hell, the Son of God endured in His own body and soul the wrath that our sins deserve. God does not blink at sin or ignore it. God dealt with it fully in His Son who received and endured an infinite punishment in our stead. Therefore we need to know that as we are, God loves us and, for

Christ's sake, accepts us. By His grace He is making us what He would have us, His sons and daughters, to be.

6. Does the teaching that God accepts us as we are minimize sin? Why not?

We talk about growing spiritually and growing in grace. We need to see that if we are to grow spiritually at all, it will be as we grow in appreciation and appropriation of the grace of God. When God received us the first time, His invitation was to come unto Him as we are; repent, believe, and He would receive us.

In the Christian life, it is just the same. When we, as His dear children sin, God invites us to come to Him in repentance, confessing our sins and believing in the graciousness of God who continues to forgive us.

7. What must we do to be forgiven of our daily sins?

If you know that you are a Christian, if you know that you are going to heaven, if you know that you are God's child, then you know that this is how you came to Christ. But since then, perhaps you have turned to your own works, trusting in them to make you acceptable to God. And now you fear to come to Him because you do not believe that you are still acceptable. My friend, you never were and you never will be acceptable to God in your own right.

25

Yet, in Christ, we are accepted though entirely un-acceptable, beloved though unlovely.

This walk in Christ has been described in many ways. Dr. Bill Bright uses a very apt metaphor when he describes it as "spiritual breathing." He feels that this is one of the most important secrets of the Christian life. We live our physical lives by breathing; by exhaling the poisonous fumes that accumulate in our bodies and by inhaling fresh, pure air.

We live spiritually in the Christian life also by breathing; that is, by exhaling—confessing our sins and repenting of them, and by inhaling—that is, by faith appropriating, claiming and taking hold of the grace of God and His forgiveness in Christ. So as a Christian goes through the day, he confesses his sins and claims anew the promises of God. He is not like Adam who, after he sinned, ran and hid beneath a tree.

8. *How does Bill Bright of Campus Crusade for Christ describe this daily walk of forgiveness with God? Describe "spiritual breathing" in your own words.*

Many Christians, especially new ones, when they sin say, "Oh, how could this be? How could I have done this against God who has done so much for me? I suppose I'm not even a Christian anymore." And so they are afraid to come into God's presence. They turn away from His Word and from prayer— the very thing the devil wants them to do. They don't want to talk to God. They're afraid that He will condemn them, so they do exactly the opposite of what they ought to do.

What should they do?

They should go immediately to a gracious Father who loves them, knowing that He will receive them and, in the name of Christ, confess their sins and claim anew His forgiveness and His refilling with the Spirit of God.

9. What is the most typical reaction of Christians, especially new Christians, when they sin? What should they do?

If we would do this, I believe we would find that we could live our lives far above anything that we have known. This does not mean that we will never sin. In fact, we will never be perfect in this life. But it does mean that when we do sin, we are not going to get into that downward spiral which takes us ever farther away from God.

Taking us away from God is what Satan wants. He would whisper to you, "Now you've done it. Now you've ruined it all. God's not going to have anything more to do with you. You had better forget all about being a Christian."

But the Bible says, "If we confess our sins, he is faithful and just to forgive us our sins, and to cleanse us from all unrighteousness" (1 John 1:9).

Many people cannot understand why they do the things they do. Perhaps they need to learn and understand more clearly the great truth of what happened to them when they became Christians.

What did happen?

The Bible teaches that when Jesus comes into our hearts, He creates a new life, a new nature within us. But this new nature does not obliterate the old. The Christian, therefore, is a unique individual in whom there dwell two natures: the old nature and the new.

The old nature can do nothing but sin. That is why the person, before he is regenerated by God, can do nothing but sin. Oh, he may be ever so righteous in the eyes of men and society. He may be ever so pious in the eyes of the church. But since his motives are wrong, and his goal is not the glory of God, everything he does is sin. He may give $10 million to the church, but God knows he is doing it only for his own pride and, therefore, it is sin. The old nature is depraved and fallen and can do nothing that is pleasing in the sight of God.

On the other hand, the new nature cannot sin at all. As John tells us in his first epistle, "Whosoever is born of God sinneth not" (1 John 5:18). This new nature does not sin. It cannot sin; it is of God. Therefore, there is in the believer these two natures and, because of this, there arises an irreconcilable warfare between them. "The flesh lusteth against the Spirit, and the Spirit against the flesh: and these are contrary the one to the other . . ." (Galatians 5:17).

Now the question is: to which nature are we going to yield ourselves? In Romans, Paul—after five chapters dealing with the great doctrine of justification—then gives his first instruction to the believer. It is this: "Neither yield your members as instruments of unrighteousness unto sin: but yield yourselves unto God . . ." (Romans 6:13).

The secret of the Christian life is letting the new nature work its way out in our lives. This has been described as having Christ sit on the throne of our hearts. When the new nature is "plugged in," so to speak, our life is going to bring forth the fruit of the Spirit. "But the fruit of the Spirit is love, joy, peace, longsuffering, gentleness, goodness, faith, meekness, temperance . . ." (Galatians 5:22,23).

When the old nature is "plugged in," there is going to come forth the works of the flesh which are strife, jealousy, animosity, hatred, lust, covetousness and greed. All of these are the works of the flesh (Galatians 5:19-21), and it depends on which nature we yield ourselves unto.

Now, how about you? Which nature is going to control your life? Your will is asking, "This one or that one?" You are answering, "Christ, I want you to control my life. I want this new nature to be expressed in my members." If you do that this day, God will bless your life abundantly.

10. Describe the two natures of a Christian. Why is it important to understand the distinction between the two?

Oh, that God would enable us to learn to yield our members unto Him, to begin today thinking, not that we have to live a whole life, but that we live just one day at a time. I hope that when you got out of bed this morning you said, "This is the day which the Lord hath made; . . . rejoice and be glad in it" (Psalm 118:24). This is what God wants. He wants us to be glad. "Rejoice in the Lord always: and again I say, Rejoice" (Philippians 4:4).

I hope that tomorrow before you even get out of bed you will commit the day unto the Lord and ask the Spirit of God to bring forth His precious fruit in your life: love, joy, peace.

Go to God and His Word. Go to Him in prayer. Pray that Christ will control your life, that He will bring forth these fruits as you have relationships with other people. Maybe someone will not be kind to you. There's an opportunity to forgive. Maybe you're going to have a trial. There's an opportunity, not for anxiety, but for trust in Christ to help you in your life. Maybe there's someone who is going to be difficult to get along with. There's an opportunity to love him for Christ's sake.

This can make every day a great adventure with God. Will you try it today? As soon as you are aware of any sin in your life—any tone of voice, any look in your eye, any attitude of your heart that is not pleasing to God, then realize that your nature is asserting itself. Confess the sin and draw in again the free Spirit of God. Ask for His mercy and His forgiveness. What a difference it will make in your day, and you will manifest Jesus Christ to others. The world is waiting to see this manifestation of Christ being realized daily in our hearts and lives and being lived out in our daily conduct.

11. What manifestation of Christ being realized daily in our hearts and lives and lived out in our conduct is the world waiting to see?

There is an incident in the book entitled *A Second Touch* where a successful executive who is a Christian had been living a defeated life for a long time. He decided one day that he was going to live this day for Christ, and he asked the Spirit of God to bring forth the fruits of the Spirit in his life.

He got out of bed and began the morning with God's Word and prayer. But he didn't get up quite early enough and so found himself rushing out of the door to catch his train downtown. As he entered the train station, he heard the last call for the train. With his briefcase in hand, he rushed across the train station and, in haste, he hit a little boy who had a big box in his hands containing a new jigsaw puzzle. The little boy spun around, and the jigsaw puzzle flew out in all directions, all over the platform.

The man looked at the train, then down at the little boy. He started to move towards his train, but then he remembered his prayer and it stopped him dead in his tracks. He put down his briefcase, got down on his knees and began to help the little boy pick up the pieces of the jigsaw puzzle.

A few minutes later, with a realization of the presence of God like he had never known before and with the joy of his salvation in his heart, he placed the last piece of the puzzle in the box. As he stood up, the little boy looked up in his face and said, "Mister, are you Jesus?"

12. *What is the main point of the story involving the successful executive and the little boy's scattered puzzle?*

31

I hope that today will be an exciting day for you, a day of walking with Christ. Let me encourage you to read again in the Gospel of John. May Christ grant you a day blessed by His love.

"Oh God, forgive us that so much of the time we are not like Thee at all—that we yield our members to anger and impatience and covetousness and lust. Oh, may Christ shine through us today as we yield our members unto Thee. And as we have received Thee, by Thy grace may we walk in Thee. And may others see Christ living in us this day. In Jesus' name. Amen."

Study Helps

1. Examine the following Scriptures in their context: 1 John 3:4; Romans 3:19; Jeremiah 31:34; Matthew 26:28; Luke 24:47; Acts 2:38; 3:19; and following; Ephesians 1:7; 1 Peter 2:24; 2 Corinthians 5:21; 1 John 1:8 and following; Psalm 90:8.

2. Study the *Westminster Confession of Faith,* Chapters 15-17: "Of Sanctification," "Of Saving Faith," "Of Repentance unto Life," "Of Good Works," and "Of the Perseverance of the Saints," in *The Confession of Faith of the Presbyterian Church in the United States*. Richmond, Virginia: The Board of Christian Education, 1965.

3. Read the following books:

Gill, Donald H. *Live, Christian, Live!* Glendale, California: Regal Books Division, G/L Publications, 1970.

Stott, John. *Confess Your Sins.* London: Hodder & Stoughton, Ltd., 1964.

Graham, Billy. *Guide for Christian Living*. Minneapolis: Billy Graham Evangelistic Association, n.d. Note Chapter 2, "Enemies of the Christian."

Calvin, John. *Golden Booklet of the True Christian Life*. Grand Rapids, Michigan: Baker Book House, 1952.

Pink, Arthur. *Doctrine of Sanctification*. Swengel, Pennsylvania: Reiner Publications, 1966.

Miller, Keith. *A Second Touch*. Waco, Texas: Word Books, 1967.

Gerstner, John H. *Theology for Everyman*. Chicago: Moody Press, 1965. Note chapter on "Santification: Christianizing the Christian."

CHAPTER 3

Getting into the Bible

I want to consider with you a very important subject, the subject of the Scriptures: the Bible.

We live in a time when the Scriptures are ridiculed by some, ignored by more, and outrightly denied by many. We live in a day when there is a vast ignorance of the Bible. In fact, one survey showed that about 60 percent of the people asked could not name the authors of the four Gospels: Matthew, Mark, Luke and John. I am convinced that the overwhelming majority of people who deny the Bible's truths do not really have the slightest idea of what the Scriptures really teach.

There are two main aspects of the Bible. First, what it teaches concerning itself. And secondly, how we can go about studying it more effectively.

Let's begin with what the Bible teaches concerning itself. Does the Scripture claim that it is inspired? Second Timothy 3:16,17 says, "All scripture is given by inspiration of God, and is profitable for doctrine, for reproof, for correction, for instruction in righteousness: that the man of God may be perfect, thoroughly furnished unto all good works." The Bible says of itself that all Scripture is given by inspiration of God.

1. Does the Bible claim that it is inspired? Where?

Before we concern ourselves with substantiating this claim, it is important that we at least note that it says, "All scripture is given by inspiration of God." The Bible claims for itself to be inspired. And it says that this inspiration is plenary; that is that all Scripture, the totality of Scripture, is inspired by God. This means not a part of it, but all of it.

So we believe in plenary inspiration or full and complete inspiration. This, therefore, does not allow one to exclude, cafeteria style, those particular parts of the Bible that do not suit one's taste. The inspiration of the Scripture includes, for example, the creation stories of Genesis as well as the miracle stories of the Gospels, the virgin birth, Jonah and his great fish, and Noah and the Flood.

I mention these as some of the portions which skeptics and unbelievers are most likely to attack and deny. But if all Scripture is given by inspiration of God, then it is either all inspired or it is not inspired. The Bible's claim is that all Scripture is given from God.

2. What is meant by plenary inspiration?

We also believe this inspiration is verbal in its nature. It is not, as some have said, merely ideas which God has inspired: the idea that God has given to men some great thoughts and left it to their own imaginations to figure out how to write them down. Of course, they say, there are many mistakes in the wording, but these are not too important for it is the thought, the ideas that count. This is a popular idea in some circles, but it will not square with the Scriptures.

The Bible says, "I have put my words in thy mouth" (Jeremiah 1:9). God spake all these words saying, "The word of the Lord hath come unto me" (Jeremiah 25:3). Over and over again we see the statement made that these are the words which are given by God and not merely the ideas. Thus we see that Scripture claims its inspiration is not only plenary, but also verbal.

3. *What is meant by verbal inspiration?*

This leads us to a third fact that the inspiration of the Scriptures renders them infallible—unable to fail or to make mistakes. It should be noted that whether or not the Scriptures are inspired is not the same question as whether or not the Scriptures are true.

There are books written today which contain truths that are not inspired. It is conceivable that there may be some book written today which is entirely true, but which is still not inspired by God. Two and two are four. That's true, but it's not inspired.

So we also should note that if the Bible is inspired, then it will be true. If it is true in things that could not be known by any human process, then this would lead us to realize that it is inspired. Truth and inspiration are two different questions, though they are related.

We have some men today who hold to what is called neo-orthodoxy. They are, as someone said, the liberal halfway home, the prodigal son halfway to his father's house. Their view is really the same old radical unbelief of the last century, draping itself in seemingly orthodox clothing and, therefore, making itself all the more deceptive.

These people speak of the Bible as being inspired, but they have something which is a novelty in their thoughts. They believe that the Bible can be inspired without being true. To the average person that is utterly unthinkable. If something has been completely inspired by the God of all truth, the God who cannot lie, the God who knows all things, the God who is omniscient, then it is evident that the Bible—His Word—would be true.

"Thy word is truth" (John 17:17), says Christ to His Father. Further, the Lord of Glory, Jesus Christ, says, "The scripture cannot be broken" (John 10:35). Therefore, the Scriptures are infallible; they are true in all their parts.

All of the statements of the Bible, all of its promises, all of its prophecies, all of its declarations are true because they are inspired by the God of truth. Therefore, we believe and so the historic, orthodox Christian faith has believed that the Bible is plenarily, verbally and infallibly inspired. The totality of the Scriptures, not only the ideas, but also the words are inspired in such a way that the Bible cannot err.

4. What is meant by infallible inspiration?

Let us see now what the word "inspired" means. There are many people today who say, "Oh, I believe the Bible is inspired as were Shakespeare, Milton and others." What they really mean is that these works are inspiring. But there is a vast difference between something being inspired and something being inspiring.

Actually the Greek word *theopneustos* which is translated "inspired," literally means "God-breathed." All Scripture is "God-breathed." According to the Bible, Scripture is the very breath of God. Scripture is breathed out by God.

When you come to the genealogical tables of the Book of Numbers, and the long series of "begats" at the beginning of Matthew, you may be completely uninspired as you read them. You may find these tables totally lacking in anything which causes your heart to beat a little faster, but they are still God-breathed. The person who is discerning and has some knowledge of biblical tools can find precious jewels even in these chapters.

The problem may not be in the Scriptures; it may be in us, if we do not find them inspiring. It is the Scriptures which the Bible primarily teaches are inspired. The Scriptures—not the apostles or the prophets, that is, the writers—but the writings.

"All scripture is given by inspiration of God" (2

Timothy 3:16). All Scripture is God-breathed. This is far different from Mozart waking up with a melody running through his mind and rushing to write it down on paper. *He* was inspired, but in the case of the Bible, it is the *Scripture* which is inspired, or rather more accurately, expired—breathed out by God. This is the Bible's claim.

5. *What do we mean when we say the Bible is inspired?*

Some say Christians believe the Bible is inspired because the Bible says it is inspired; therefore the Bible is inspired. This is reasoning in a circle and, therefore, is not a valid argument. What shall we say to that? We say that's absolutely correct. It is arguing in a circle, and it is an invalid argument. But this is not the way Christians argue. It is the way skeptics *say* Christians argue.

Even though we do not base our claim merely on the fact that the Scriptures state they are inspired, let us remember that the Bible does, in fact, claim to be inspired by God. This is an important consideration. What, for example, if the Bible did not claim to be inspired by God? What if it was absolutely silent on the whole subject? What if it actually denied that it was inspired by God? Then it would be a far different case. But over two thousand times the Bible does claim to be inspired by God.

Throughout Scripture, from one end to the other, we read, "Thus saith the Lord" (Exodus 4:22); "The word of the Lord came unto the prophet" (2

Samuel 24:11); "The Spirit of the Lord spake by me" (2 Samuel 23:2); "The word of the Lord came unto me, saying" (Zechariah 4:8); "Hear ye the word of the Lord" (2 Kings 7:1); "Thus saith the Lord God of Israel" (Exodus 32:27). Throughout Scripture, from Genesis to Revelation, there is this pervasive fact of God speaking which cannot be ignored.

The Scriptures claim on almost every page that the Bible from beginning to end, from Genesis to Revelation, is the Word of the living God revealed to man. This is not some isolated saying that appears once or twice and that may be overlooked or interpreted in some clever way. This claim of being God's Word is everywhere in the Bible. It is a ubiquitous concept found throughout the entirety of the Scriptures. Therefore, if the Bible is not truly God's Word, it means the men who wrote it were deluded or deceived, and their high and elevated teachings must now be looked at in an entirely different light. Therefore, we must begin with the important fact that the Bible claims to be inspired.

We know there are people who claim to speak for God, but the fact of such a claim does not substantiate it. Many people will say, "Well, after all, isn't it true that the Bible was written simply by men? What is so different about that?"

Indeed, what is so different?

This question reminds me of a tourist in South Africa standing before the entrance to the wealthiest diamond mine the world has ever known. "Well," he says, "what's so different about that? It's just a hole in the ground, just like any other hole in the ground." But the men who go down and see the vast precious wealth of that mine would say, "You fool! All that you have in this world could not purchase this mine. It is of inestimable value." And so is the Bible.

Is the Word of God just a book written by men? No. The Bible *verifies* its claim of inspiration and even tells us how we can do so. You don't have to devise means of discovering whether this frequently repeated claim of inspiration is true or not. God tells you the way to find out. He says that hereby you shall know if a prophet has been sent by Me, if he speaks for Me; he shall prophesy the future, and it shall come to pass. (See Jeremiah 28:9.)

This declaration is not to be understood to mean a few isolated prophecies which are partly right and partly wrong. Anybody can guess, even guess right part of the time. But the Bible claims there are a vast number of prophecies which infallibly will come to pass.

6. How does the Bible verify its claim to be the inspired Word of the living God?

These prophecies concern the very center of the teaching of the Bible—the main personage about whom the Scriptures were written. That Person, of course, is Jesus of Nazareth, the Messiah of God, the Saviour of the world. Here the amazing wisdom of God is seen. The Old and the New Testaments are divided by over 400 years. The Old Testament was written between approximately 1400 B.C. and 400 B.C. After that it was translated into Greek

41

called the Septuagint version. This version was completed in about 150 B.C. There could be no possible doubt that the Old Testament Hebrew Scriptures were completed hundreds of years before Christ was born. The New Testament was written during the first century A.D.

One of the great functions of the Old Testament was to promise that a Messiah was to come in the fulness of time to redeem mankind. But how could this Messiah be identified? The identification would be done in this way: various facets of His life would be prophesied forming a picture of the Messiah. Then when He came the picture could be put together, and He could be identified. The prophecies are like the pieces of a jigsaw puzzle, except that each piece contains a complete event, not just the portion of one. In themselves, the individual prophecies do not mean much, but when you put them all together, they form a perfect picture.

7. What is one of the great functions of the Old Testament? How was this identification to be made?

The Old Testament contains 333 prophecies concerning the coming of Jesus Christ alone, as well as hundreds of other prophecies. No other book in the world even purports to do such a thing as this. There is no other person in the world whose life has been so minutely described in all of its details long before He was born.

Can you imagine someone similarly prophesying the life of Abraham Lincoln? To equal the biblical

42

prophecies about Christ, they would have had to describe not only the nation in which Lincoln was born, but also the state and the city of his birth. They would have had to describe his parents, his grandparents, his great-great-great-great-great-grandparents and trace his lineage back through the centuries.

In addition, they would have had to describe the character he would have, the conduct he would exhibit, the life he would live, and the offices he would hold. In minute detail, they would have had to describe all the events of his ministry.

They would also have had to describe where he would live, where he would minister, what his family and friends would think about him, and how his life would end. They would have had to describe not only that he would be assassinated, but also that he would be shot in the head.

They would have had to do all this no later than A.D. 1350, and then they would have had to *add approximately 320 other details of his life.*

And so it is, through tiny pieces of prophecy, some 333 of them, we see—when they are fitted together—a perfect mosaic that describes and pictures Jesus Christ so intimately, so perfectly that those who have carefully examined it cannot help but be impressed by it.

A few of the facts about the coming Messiah that are foretold in the Old Testament (which ends about 400 B.C.) are: The Messiah would come through the seed of a woman, not of a man. He would be born of the lineage of Abraham, of the ancestry of Isaac, and of the line of Jacob. He would come at a certain set time, and He would come to the second Temple which was destroyed in A.D. 70.

The Messiah would come out of the tribe of Judah. (No Jew can prove today that He is of the tribe of Judah because all of the chronological tables were destroyed by Titus and Vespasian in A.D. 70.) He would also be descended from David. (There is also no Jew living today who can prove he is a descendant of David.)

Furthermore, the Bible describes the very date on which Christ would be born: He would come 483 years after the decree went out from Artaxerxes after the Babylonian captivity to rebuild the Temple. We are told in Scripture that Christ would be born of a virgin, and that He would be born in the city of Bethlehem in the state of Judea. Great persons would come to adore Him. He would come suddenly to His Temple. He would be preceded by John the Baptist, would be anointed with the Holy Spirit, and would be a prophet like unto Moses.

The Scriptures prophesied that Christ would enter into a public ministry, would begin it in Galilee, and would preach publicly in Jerusalem.

Of His character, the Old Testament tells us that He would be stricken with poverty, that He would be meek and lacking in ostentation. He would be tender and compassionate. He would work miracles. He would be without guile. He would bear the reproach of those about Him, would be rejected by His own brothers, would be hated without cause and would be rejected finally by the Jewish rulers.

Jews and Gentiles would combine to destroy

Jesus. He would be betrayed by His own friend with whom He had eaten, and His disciples would forsake Him. He would be sold for thirty pieces of silver, and His price would be given for a potter's field. He would be spit upon, scourged and nailed to a cross.

Not only would Christ be forsaken by His friends, He would be forsaken by God. He would be mocked by priests and given gall and vinegar to drink. His suffering would be intense, but His suffering would be vicarious. And He would be silent midst all of His tortures. His garments would be parted, and lots cast for His vesture. He would be numbered with the transgressors, yet He would make intercession for those who murdered Him.

The Scriptures further tell us His death would be among thieves. Not a bone of Him would be broken, but His hands and His feet would be pierced. He would be buried with the rich, but His flesh would not see corruption because He would arise from the dead, ascend into Heaven, and sit at the right hand of God. And then His gospel would be preached unto the Gentiles, and His rest would be glorious.

Add to all these some three hundred more prophecies, and you have the life of Jesus Christ as pictured in the Old Testament. Only the high points of the mountains have been touched. Nowhere else in all the world, in all the history of man, has anything such as this ever been known. "Only a book written by mere men!" Only a mere man ignorant of what the Book of God really contains would speak such words.

8. Why are the Old Testament prophecies about Christ important today?

Having seen something of the inspiration and nature of the Scripture, let us now consider how to study the Word of God. We need to remember that this Book is different from any other book written in this world. It is the living, quickening, life-giving Word of God.

The Bible says, "As newborn babes, desire the sincere milk of the word, that ye may grow thereby" (1 Peter 2:2). We are to study it. We are to meditate upon it. We are to hide it in our hearts, to memorize it, and God will use it to transform our lives.

No doubt you have already begun to study the Gospel of John. This is a good place to begin. When you have finished John, go on to read the epistle to the Romans, the central epistle of the New Testament.

There are various types of reading in the Bible. It's not simply a book; it's a whole library. But for the moment, it is probably best if you confine yourself to the New Testament and the book of John.

In studying the Scriptures, it is important to set aside a certain time each day, preferably in the morning, so that God can use it to bless your life as you begin the day. This is better, I feel, than at the end of the day when "the horse has already escaped the barn," as it were, and you have already managed to mess up that day. Better to begin in the morning with His Word and with prayer.

As you select the passage to read, you should come to it expectantly, believingly, and praying that God the Holy Spirit will enlighten your mind to understand and receive the Word He has for you. Remember that you are coming to the Word of the living God; to a God who delights to bless your life, who has something for you every day and who wants to speak to you. God speaks to us through His Word, and we speak to Him through prayer.

9. *What are some basic principles to remember before you begin to study the Word of God, the Bible?*

Now, after you read a portion of Scripture—a few verses or a chapter—it's good first of all to develop the habit of observation, of really looking at what you have read. Too often people read through a passage and then get up and go away, hardly knowing at all what they have read.

Try to observe. You will find it a helpful habit to keep a notebook and to indicate what chapter of Scripture you have read and what you have observed.

The great scientist Agassiz, who was one of the greatest naturalists in the world, used to stress strongly that his students learn the art of observation. Agassiz gave one young man an assignment to observe everything he could about a frog. He looked at the frog for about a half hour, wrote down everything he saw and then came back to Agassiz and said, "What do I do now?"

"Look at it some more," replied Agassiz.

The young man went back and another hour went by, and the same command was repeated. The whole day passed, and then another day, and another, and a fourth, until finally the student discovered there was a vast amount about this specimen that he had not noticed at all.

And so, as you go over and over the Scriptures, you are going over ground which is tremendously wealthy, ground in which are buried all sorts of precious gems. Read carefully and note carefully what you read.

10. Define "observation."

After you have observed as much as you can about the text, the second thing to do is to interpret what the Scripture says. Every person is responsible to interpret the Bible. There are, however, some basic hermeneutical or interpretive principles that you should understand.

The Bible is its own interpreter. Difficult passages are often explained in context or in other places in Scripture. A text without a context is a pretext. Some people say the Bible can be made to say anything you want it to say. This is true, if you ignore the principles of interpretation.

For example, the Bible says "Then Judas . . . went and hanged himself," "go, and do thou likewise," and "that thou doest, do quickly" (Matthew 27:3,5; Luke 10:37; John 13:27). Now the Bible actually says that. But it says it in three different places, in three entirely different contexts about three completely different situations. The Bible doesn't mean at all what these verses mean when wrongly combined in this way. So we need to consider certain principles in our interpretations.

First of all, ask yourself, *"What does the text really say?"* Always look at the text very carefully and don't come to some false conclusion as to what it says. Many people hastily suppose the Bible says something which it really doesn't say. For example, how many times have you heard it stated, "The Bible teaches that money is the root of all evil"? There are many people who would swear the Bible says this. Yet what it actually says is, "The *love* (italics added) of money is the root of all evil . . ." (1 Timothy 6:10). There is quite a difference in the meaning.

The second principle beyond the text itself deals with *"the immediate context"* which helps to throw light on the meaning of the text; to see the jewel in its setting where God has placed it, so that we might better understand what the text really means.

Thirdly, there is what is known as the *"whole analogy of Scripture;"* that is, the total context of the entire Bible. To repeat, the Bible explains itself, and if something is obscure in one place, there will be other places where it speaks more clearly. Therefore, you should learn how to use a *concordance*, and to be able to look up different passages in the Bible.

After interpreting a text as best you can yourself, it would be well to get a good *commentary* which will help you in interpreting the Scripture further. You need, however, to be careful not to rely only on the commentary and fail to do your own interpreting and searching of Scripture first. There are many good commentaries, and there are some that are not so good. *Matthew Henry's Commentary* has stood the test of time and is acclaimed as being one of the best. I think you will find it to be a great help in your Bible study.

11. Define "interpretation." What are the three interpretive principles?

Fourthly, there is the matter of *application*. We're not simply to read Scripture, then to go our way and forget it. We are to apply it to ourselves. But what does this mean? It means that there are certain things for which you should be on the lookout, things you might want to underline. And don't be afraid to mark your Bible. Some people use colored pencils or make notes in the margin so that their Bibles will be more helpful to *them*.

One thing you should look for is a promise or *promises from God*. If you find that there is a promise, that God promises He will do something, you should underline it. In fact, it's a good practice to learn the promises of God. It has been stated that our whole life at its conclusion will be seen to be simply an unfolding of God's fulfillment of the promises which He has made. Yet many of us fail to live our lives to the fullest because we do not claim the promises that God has made to us. These are like uncashed checks. They are there for our taking, but we need to learn them, and we need to claim them by faith, to trust God for them.

You have trusted Christ for your eternal salvation, and He has assured you He will take you to be with Him in heaven. Now you must learn to trust Him for temporal things as well, for the material things of this life, for every aspect of your life. God is concerned with the smallest detail; even "the very hairs of your head are all numbered" (Matthew 10:30). You want to learn to trust Him for your family, for your business, for your children, for your finances, for every decision, for every need. Learn to rest upon Him. Learn the secret of spiritual serenity—and this you will learn, in great part, by learning to rely upon the promises of God.

There may also be a *commandment* in the passage for you to obey. You will want to mark this as well. This is something for you to heed, for you to obey. If you truly love Christ, you will want to keep His commandments. (See John 14:21.) And as you do, you will realize that He is wise and loving and that His commandments are not burdensome, but are given simply to make our lives the richest and fullest possible.

If you are a parent, you know that the commandments you give your children come out of a heart of love and are designed as best you know for their well-being. God has infinite love and total knowledge; therefore, one of the great secrets you need to learn is that fulness of life will come, not in disobeying His commandments, but in obeying them.

Finally, there may be some *example* for you to follow. The Scriptures are filled with examples; some bad, some good, but they are examples from which you can learn. There are many great, godly men and women whose examples can be an encouragement and an inspiration to you.

12. Define "application." What is a promise of God? Give an example. What is a commandment of God? Give an example. What purpose do examples serve in the Bible?

All of these things will help your daily time of Scripture reading, study and meditation to be a time of rich blessing and fulfillment in your life, rather than a duty to perform. I trust that as you read the Word of God today and throughout the rest of your life, He will make it a continuing and ever more exciting adventure with Him. God bless you as you go through this day, resting upon His eternal Word.

"Gracious Father, Thy Word is truth. Heaven and earth shall pass away, but not one jot or tittle of Thy Word shall ever pass away. Lord, may it be that we will learn that the Saviour who was revealed in the Scripture desires to bless our lives; that He loves us and wants this day to be an abundant one with Him. And may we learn that this blessing in great part comes through His Word. Teach us to love it, learn it, and live by it. For Christ's sake. Amen."

Study Helps

1. Look up the following Old Testament prophecies on Christ and read them in their context: Genesis 3:15; 17:19; 18:18; 49:10; Numbers 24:17; Deuteronomy 18:15; Psalms 2:2; 16:10; 22;16,18; 34:20;

41:9; 68:18; 69:4,21; 132:11; Isaiah 7:14,15; 9:1,2,6,7; 42:6; 50:6; 52:13,14; 53:1-12; 59:20; 60:3; 61:1,2; Daniel 7:13,14; 9:25,26; Micah 5:2; Zechariah 9:9; 11:12,13; 12:10; Malachi 3:1.

2. Examine in their context the references in the following list of subjects on the Bible:

All Scripture is God-breathed (2 Timothy 3:16).

It cannot be broken and shall not pass away (John 10:34; Matthew 5:18,19).

Scripture is the mouthpiece of God the Holy Spirit (Hebrews 3:7; Matthew 22:43; Acts 4:25).

The words of God are placed in the mouth of His servants the prophets (Jeremiah 1:9; 1 Corinthians 2:13).

The prime author of Scripture is the Holy Spirit. The human authors are His instruments in conveying a message of divine authority. God does not lie (Proverbs 30:5,6; Numbers 23:19), and He insists that His children do not lie either (Exodus 20:16; Psalm 63:11).

Divine truthfulness is the rock beneath biblical infallibility (Page 10 of *A Defense of Biblical Infallibility* by Clark H. Pinnock).

3. Read these additional Scriptures:

1 Corinthians 2:10-14; Hebrews 1:1,2; Galatians 1:11,12; 2 Peter 1:20,21; 3:15,16; John 16:13,14.

4. Study the *Westminster Confession of Faith,* Chapter 1: "Of the Holy Scripture," of *The Confession of Faith of the Presbyterian Church in the United States.* Richmond, Virginia: The Board of Christian Education, 1965.

5. Read the following books:

Mears, Henrietta C. *A Look at the Old Testament.*

Glendale, California: Regal Books Division, G/L Publications, 1966.

Mears, Henrietta C. *A Look at the New Testament*. Glendale, California: Regal Books Division, G/L Publications, 1966.

Mears, Henrietta C. *What the Bible Is All About*. Glendale, California: Regal Books Division, G/L Publications, 1966.

Young, Edward J. *Thy Word Is Truth*. Grand Rapids, Michigan: William B. Eerdmans Publishing Company, 1957.

Lloyd-Jones, David Martyn. *Authority*. Downers Grove, Illinois: Inter-Varsity Press, 1967. Note Chapter 2, "The Authority of the Scriptures."

Spurgeon, Charles H. *How to Read the Bible*. London: Evangelical Press, n.d. Distributed by Puritan-Reformed Book Club, Wilmington, Delaware.

Graham, Billy. *Peace with God*. Garden City, New York: Doubleday & Co., Inc., 1953. Note Chapter 2, "The Bible."

Pinnock, Clark H. *A Defense of Biblical Infallibility*. Nutley, New Jersey: Presbyterian and Reformed Publishing Company, 1971.

CHAPTER 4

Practicing the Art of Prayer

We have considered the importance of Scripture and how God speaks to man. Now I would like us to consider the other half of that dialogue—how we speak to God.

Our text is James 1:3: "Knowing this, that the trying of your faith worketh patience."

Men with empty water bottles stagger over burning desert sands. They die, and their bones bleach in the blazing sun, while nearby palm trees grow and flourish. But the hot winds that sift sand over their bleached bones only cause the green branches of those trees to flutter in the breeze because the trees have roots which reach down and take hold of unseen fountains below.

So it is today in the deserts of our modern cities, where many perish and are consumed in the noontime heat and pressures of daily life. The anxieties of life—making a living, tensions of the office, the pressures of home and the difficulty of family life in a modern world—all contribute to wither the soul and bring many to the end of themselves and total ruin.

However, at the same time, in the same city deserts, others smile and seem to float through their problems on a river of serenity that causes onlookers to be utterly amazed. But if you look deep into those smiling eyes, you will see in their souls the luxuriant growth that comes only where roots have taken hold of hidden fountains beneath. The fountain that we are considering primarily is the fountain of communion with the living God. He is the Water of Life who will make a living fountain to spring up in our souls. This communion with the living God, the Fount of Life, is called prayer.

Prayer is not only a universal instinct, it is also an art. As theology is the queen of the sciences, prayer is the noblest of the arts, surpassing music, painting and sculpture. The divine art of prayer is personal linkage with the Eternal. It is communion with power unseen which transforms lives in ways that are absolutely unaccountable when one looks at the desert winds which blow about our modern world.

1. What is prayer? Why is it called an art?

Have you yet learned this art? None of us has learned it as we ought. But the greatest of God's men and women have always been men and women who have learned the art of prayer. Our great exemplar, the Son of God Himself, was preeminently a man of prayer. He rose up often long before daylight and went out into a mountain alone to pray.

Repeatedly we see Christ in a lonely mountain place at night spending long hours of solitude with His Father.

2. Who is our great example in prayer? What element characterized His prayer time?

One of the greatest reasons for the rise of mental illness in the nation today is a lack of personal prayer. I say that without any fear of contradiction, for the Scripture says, "Be careful (or anxious) for nothing; but in every thing by prayer and supplication with thanksgiving let your requests be made known unto God. And the peace of God, which passeth all understanding, shall keep your hearts and minds through Christ Jesus" (Philippians 4:6,7).

If our requests with thanksgiving are not made, and our eyes are not fixed upon the Christ of perfect peace, then our hearts indeed will be filled with anxiety. They will be torn this way and that. And this is exactly what has driven the many persons into mental depressions and breakdowns who fill the asylums of this country. And there are vast millions of others that never enter mental hospitals but who live lives of joylessness, peacelessness and anxiety because of their lack of personal prayer.

3. Why are many hearts filled with anxiety? What is God's remedy according to Philippians 4:6,7?

Prayer is the most needed art in our times. It is also a most difficult art. It is often said that "Satan trembles when he sees the weakest saint upon his knees." But he does more than tremble. He uses all of his wiles to keep us from prayer. And so he uses the pressure of the world, the crowd of the daily schedule and the tyranny of the urgent to keep us from the place of quiet rest, and thus our souls find no solitude.

4. What things have hindered many people from prayer?

We are not strengthened because we do not wait before the Lord. We do not rise up with wings and fly because we do not kneel down in prayer and wait.

Satan uses many a wile, many a deceit, many a device to keep us from prayer. What artifice of his has been most successful with you? What trick has he used to keep you from prayer?

5. What means has Satan used to keep you from prayer?

"Lord, teach us to pray" (Luke 11:1) was the heart cry of the disciples as they looked at Him who lived in perfect communion with the living God.

What are some of the basic elements that we are to learn if we are to master this art of prayer? Probably you have tried to learn some art in your lifetime. I remember the many hours that I spent as a little fellow learning to play the clarinet and saxophone. How my parents endured it, I will never know!

If we are persistent and persevere, we shall one day master our art. Someone said, "If you will just spend a little time each day doing most anything, in due process you will become an expert at it." It doesn't matter what field it is, you can learn more than most, if you will stick with it every day.

But how does one learn an art?

First, there must be a desire to learn. Whether it be painting or playing the guitar, there must first be that desire. Then, if you really want to learn, the next thing you must do is obtain an instructor. The Lord Jesus Christ is the perfect teacher.

You will also need an instruction book. The Scriptures are the perfect source of instruction on this matter of prayer. Many people who make reference to prayer indicate when they do so that their own concept of prayer is not founded on biblical principles. They have made up their own theology, and it is no wonder that they end up in utter frustration. The Bible has a great deal to say about prayer, and if we ignore what it says, we might as well not pray at all.

6. Who is our teacher in the art of prayer? Where are His instructions found?

There are also many other books which have collated the scriptural teachings on prayer and expounded upon them. They too will be of considerable help to you in learning the art of prayer.

Prayer consists of certain basic elements. And unquestionably, one of these is confession. We come before an all Holy God whose eyes are so pure He

59

"canst not look on iniquity" (Habakkuk 1:13). Therefore, any genuine understanding of God and ourselves will require that we approach Him with the confession of our sins and a sense of being totally unworthy to come into His presence. Further we must not be satisfied with a general confession of our sins but should confess and repent of particular sins particularly.

7. How must we approach God in prayer?

Secondly, there is the element of thanksgiving—thanking God for all that He has done for us. This changes the attitude of the soul from sour to sweet. What a blessing it is to see a holy contentment with our lot in life. So many people, because of the emptiness of their souls, are constantly grasping and reaching out for something else, not realizing that "things" will never fill the emptiness within them.

"In every human heart," Pascal said, "there is a God-shaped vacuum," and naught can fill it but God alone. Yet there continues this restless searching instead, for something else to fill that emptiness within.

As St. Augustine put it so many centuries ago, "Thou hast made us for Thyself, and our hearts are restless until they find their rest in Thee." Yet how few people today have a thankfulness and a holy contentment about their lives.

8. What attitude of prayer changes the attitude of our soul from sour to sweet?

There is a sense in which we should have a holy discontentment, but that discontentment should be with our own spiritual progress. Have you recently considered your own dissatisfaction with the state of your soul?

One of the tragedies of the Church in our day is that instead of having a holy contentment with our lot in life and a holy dissatisfaction with our spiritual progress, we find that just the opposite is the case. So many of us are complacent about the condition of our souls, yet we are anxious for the things of this world to fill our emptiness. We are dissatisfied and discontented with other things in life.

We who are complacent about our spiritual condition will give evidence of this when we rise to complain about some physical something or other that we have or have not.

The object of your discontentment will tell a great deal about your soul and your spiritual state. About what are you discontent?

9. *What is it good to be discontent about in our lives? About what are you discontent?*

A third element in prayer is petition. We are to ask God for things for ourselves. Any lawful, honest need is a reasonable request to be made in prayer. If we have made progress in prayer, we will find these petitions will have to do primarily with our spiritual growth.

It is not wrong to bring physical need to God in prayer, as He is concerned for the very hairs upon our heads. (See Matthew 10.30.) However, as

61

progress is made in the school of prayer, we will concern ourselves more with other things. We will also come to realize that our Father in heaven knows we "have need of these things" (Luke 12:30).

10. What is a third element of prayer? What things may we ask for?

A fourth element is intercession. As we move into the college level of prayer, we begin to pray for other people. The needs of this world are vast. Jesus was the Great Intercessor. Paul was a great intercessor. Often even when in prison Paul prayed for others.

How much do you really pray for others? How much do you agonize in prayer for other people? When did you last weep for someone else? When did we last cry over the lostness of another person —even of one that you say you love? "He that goeth forth and *weepeth*, bearing precious seed, shall doubtless come again with rejoicing, bringing his sheaves with him" (Psalm 126:6).

Pray for your minister. Pray for those who have the rule over you. Pray for the world. Pray for peace. And pray for lost people with whom you rub shoulders each day. There may be some in your family who do not yet know Christ. You should pray each day for them that they will come to discover what you have discovered.

11. What is the fourth element of prayer? For what do you pray?

The fifth element of prayer is adoration—the least exercised form of prayer. This is not merely thanking God for what He has given us but praising Him for what He is. And yet, how little of our prayers consist of adoration. Rather, much of our prayer is selfish, petty, unspiritual and carnal.

12. What is the fifth element of prayer? What does this mean to you?

The Bible also lays down certain conditions for prayer. Not every prayer will be answered. If we come to God and ask for something, we should first see what God has said about the kind of prayers He will hear and answer.

First of all, the Bible requires a right relationship with God before we can expect that our prayers will be answered. This means we must be saved and not lost. We must be His children and not the children of the devil. There is not just one great family in this world, as some would have us to believe. There are two—the children of God and the children of Satan. Jesus said of the Pharisees, "Ye are of your father the devil" (John 8:44).

We must be adopted into the family of God— born again into His family. We must be regenerated; we must be justified, repenting of our sins and by faith receiving Jesus Christ into our hearts. Then, and only then, do we enter into a right relationship with God and become His child. Otherwise, the Bible says we are at enmity with God (see Romans 5:10), we are outlaws, rebels against heaven.

Why should we expect God to answer our prayers when we continue daily to rebel against His teachings? It is somewhat like John Dillinger, the runaway outlaw, calling the police to complain about the noise next door, demanding that something be done about it and that right away. The police would have one message for him: "Surrender. Give yourself up." It is only when we surrender ourselves to God and give ourselves up to His will that we can go to Him as our Father and make requests in prayer.

13. What is the first condition of biblical prayer? Why is this important?

Secondly, the Bible sets forth the condition of a right relationship with others as having an important bearing on our prayer. The Scripture says that "if thou bring thy gift to the altar, and there rememberest that thy brother hath ought against thee; leave there thy gift before the altar, and go thy way; first be reconciled to thy brother, and then come and offer thy gift" (Matthew 5:23,24). The Bible makes this particularly true in our families. Husbands, if you are out of harmony with your wives, the Bible says your prayers will be hindered. And that goes for wives as well. (See Ephesians 5:20-25; Colossians 3:17-19.)

14. What is the second condition of biblical prayer? Why is this important?

Thirdly, the Bible says if we regard iniquity in

our heart the Lord will not hear us. If there is any sin that we are harboring in our hearts, that we have not repented of, that we are not willing to forsake, God says He will not hear our prayers.

15. What is the third condition of biblical prayer? Why is this important?

Fourthly, we must ask in faith. The Bible says, "But let him ask in faith, nothing wavering. For he that wavereth is like a wave of the sea driven with the wind and tossed. For let not that man think that he shall receive any thing of the Lord. A double minded man is unstable in all his ways" (James 1:6-8).

16. What is the fourth condition of biblical prayer? Why is this so important?

Fifthly, we must ask according to God's will. We cannot expect our Father to give us everything that we ask. It would be chaos if God were suddenly to grant all the prayers of all His children. If for one twenty-four-hour period the Lord answered all our prayers affirmatively, the world would be in such utter chaos it could never be put back together again. Thank God we can say, "Not my will, but thine, be done" (Luke 22:42).

17. What is the fifth condition of biblical prayer? Why is this important?

There are many obstacles that keep people from

praying. I think the greatest of these is disbelief. We just do not believe that God will answer our prayers. The source of this disbelief is often in prayers which we have made, but which were not answered, because we prayed them neither according to His will nor meeting the conditions of prayer.

Another obstacle to prayer is carnality—a failure to realize when we don't pray we are not spiritual men. There is also the matter of insincerity. "The cardinal virtue of prayer," said one, "is sincerity." This means to be absolutely honest, ruthlessly honest with ourselves and with God.

18. What are some obstacles that keep people from prayer? What are some obstacles that keep you from prayer?

Now, if we have a teacher, and we have a textbook, and we get the basic principles of the art of prayer, we must then set a definite time each day for practice. It is not enough for a child to run past a piano and tinkle a few notes; he must sit down and practice. This is why so few people make progress in prayer and why few are really men and women of prayer. They say they can't pray aloud, but this is merely an excuse to cover up the fact that they can't really pray at all.

Any man or woman who diligently spends much time in prayer alone, unless he is mute, can pray aloud. The person who can't pray aloud is a person who has no real closeted time of prayer, who has not learned the secrets of prayer in private.

19. Why is the practice of prayer so important? What has been your habit?

Certainly the time of prayer needs to begin in the morning. "Give us this day our daily bread" is hardly a prayer to be saved until night time.

Lastly, there needs to be a progressive practice of prayer. A piano student has a whole set of music books. He begins with the most elementary and then goes on to the most difficult piece of music. He cannot play the same tune over and over again and expect to grow in the art. But this is exactly what happens to many people in prayer. I know people who have been Christians for years, yet they still pray the same little prayer over and over again. There is no progress in their prayer life, no stretching of the soul.

If we would grow in the art of prayer, we need to have progressive prayer. We need to learn what it really means to be an intercessor. We need to know what faith in prayer really means. We need to trust God for greater things. We need to step out and up to higher levels of prayer.

20. Why is a progressive practice of prayer needed?

To be really proficient in the art of prayer is the most noble, the most needed and the most difficult of arts. It is also the most rewarding. How greatly God answers prayer. Tennyson said, "More things are wrought by prayer than this world dreams of."

How true this is! I am certain the unbelieving world which rushes around trying to knit up the raveled ends of a hectic life would be astonished if they saw how many Christians float through their problems on a river of prayer with a minimum of anxiety or concern. I heard recently the testimony of a man who had the lot of raising six children by himself. He did it, he said, with the greatest of ease. The Lord took care of them, and they just seemed to float through all the problems such a situation would bring. He committed it all to the Lord each day, and somehow it just worked.

Last year in our week of prayer here at the church, we prayed to God that ten people would give their lives for full-time Christian service in the coming year. On December 30, someone called long distance and told me he had decided to go into full-time Christian service. That was the tenth family for the year. God does indeed answer the prayers of His family.

How much are you missing, or how much have you missed by not praying as you should? Suppose the president of our country sent you a personal letter saying he was concerned about your life and wanted to help you. Suppose also he had placed in a national bank a vast sum of money for your disposal and said he wanted to provide for all of the needs of your life, and that all his powers were available to you. Would you spurn such an invitation? Of course not. Yet many of us have spurned a far more wonderful invitation from the God of all of the universe who invites us to come and "take the water of life freely" (Revelation 22:17). Ask of Him who freely gives, and He will provide for all our needs out of His riches in glory.

I hope you will begin each day with Christ in secret prayer, reaching down to those same refreshing waters and finding a new dimension to your life.

"Tomorrow and through all the tomorrows of our life, O Father, help us to pray. Make us men and women of prayer. Make us spiritual men and spiritual women whose roots reach down to the unseen fountains of living water in the quiet hours spent with Thee. In Jesus' name. Amen."

Study Helps

1. Examine these Bible passages on prayer in their context: Matthew 6:9-15; Philippians 4:6; John 15:7; 16:23,24; Romans 8:26; Hebrews 4:14-16; 1 John 4:14,15; 1 Timothy 2:1,2; James 1:5-8.

2. Study the *Westminster Confession of Faith: The Larger Catechism,* Questions 178-196, in *The Confession of Faith of the Presbyterian Church in the United States.* Richmond, Virginia: The Board of Christian Education, 1965.

3. Read the following books:

Spurgeon, C. H. *Effective Prayer.* London: Evangelical Press, n.d. Distributed by Puritan Reformed Book Club, Wilmington, Delaware.

Murray, Andrew. *With Christ in the School of Prayer.* Old Tappan, New Jersey: Fleming H. Revell Co., 1953.

Rinker, Rosalind. *Prayer: Conversing with God.* Grand Rapids, Michigan: Zondervan Publishing House, 1959.

Quiet Time: Guidebook of Devotions. Downers Grove, Illinois: Inter-Varsity Press, 1945.

Tozer, A. W. and others. *Essays on Prayer: A HIS Reader on Conversing with God.* Downers Grove, Illinois: Inter-Varsity Press, 1968.

CHAPTER 5

Continuing in Fellowship (Koinonia)

Fellowship is another subject of great importance to the Christian. Christian fellowship or *koinonia*, as it is called in the Greek text of the New Testament, is a very special sort of thing.

Our text is 1 John 1:3. Here we read, "That which we have seen and heard declare we unto you, that ye also may have fellowship with us: and truly our fellowship is with the Father, and with his Son Jesus Christ."

As we consider the vitality and virility of the Apostolic Church, that young body of Christians which burst forth into a decadent Roman world with such overwhelming power and strength, we note that one of the keys of its tremendously bold witness for Christ was *koinonia* or fellowship.

"And they continued steadfastly in the apostles' doctrine and fellowship, and in breaking of bread, and in prayers. . . . And all that believed were to-gether . . ." (Acts 2:42,44).

1. What was one of the keys to the first century Christians' bold witness for Christ? What is meant by the term "koinonia"? (Read Acts 2:41-47; 4:23-37).

Koinonia is a Greek word and yet it is one that is being used more and more in English. I think that before long it will become, as have so many bor-rowed words, part of the *lingua franca* of English. I have read it so many times recently, for there are now books on *koinonia*. And there are *koinonia* so-cieties, *koinonia* groups, even *koinonia* materials.

Koinonia will soon be a word familiar to all Christians. In a very definite sense, it means fellow-ship. It comes from a root which means to have a part in, to share in, to participate in.

One of the most distinguishing characteristics of the Early Church was this vital fellowship or *koin-onia* which they shared. We read of the Early Church that "they continued steadfastly in the apos-tles' doctrine and fellowship" (Acts 2:42). I think we need very much today to regrasp the meaning of this fellowship. If ever a generation needed it, ours does.

We live in a depersonalized world; an automated universe where men must remember their area code, their zip code, their social security number and their license plate. Now even their income tax is checked by computer. In most colleges, students are known only by a number. Seldom is their name known or is there any real concern with their lives. Truly there is a great need for real fellowship today.

I think that perhaps this is one of the secrets of the Communists' success: the fact that they have made men into comrades. Men secretly seek for some form of camaraderie, some sort of fellowship. But though Marx can make men comrades, only Christ can make them brothers.

I believe, however, that the Church has failed to enter into many of the things God meant us to enter into. We have claimed very little of the land God has promised to us. We have failed to enter into the meaning of the depth and fellowship that Christ meant for us to know.

So let us look at what is meant by this type of fellowship. It means a sharing of life. It means there is one life which is flowing through all those that live in Christ Jesus. The Early Church was very much aware that in some secret, mysterious way they had been made one. They were one temple, though many living stones; one vine, though many branches; one family, though many children. They had one life which pulsed through each of their hearts. In this confluence of life they discovered something that made their lives rich and meaningful.

We know the Early Church in Jerusalem went to the extreme of sharing all their goods in a communal type of life. They sold all they had and shared it with each other. "And all that believed were together, and had all things common; and sold their possessions and goods, and parted them to all men, as every man had need" (Acts 2:44,45).

2. What truth caused the Early Church to consider themselves to be "one"? What did they all have in common?

This communality of the Early Church is sometimes mistaken for an early form of Christian communism, and many have taken it as a pretense for advocating that the Bible teaches communism. But what the Bible teaches is completely different from communism.

The Bible teaches the private ownership of property, the first and greatest evil in the eyes of Communists. For example, Peter said to Ananias, "Whiles it remained, was it not thine own? and after it was sold, was it not in thine own power?" (Acts 5:4). While Peter's property remained his own, it was his to do what he willed with it. Communism, on the other hand, teaches that all property belongs to the State.

Secondly, the property of the Jerusalem Christians was given, not to the State, but to the Church. Now if there is anything that is completely foreign to the ideology flowing from Moscow or Peking, it is the idea that everybody ought to give everything they have to the Church. If that is communism, Marx would turn over in his grave!

Thirdly, and most important of all, the giving was voluntary. And this alone sets Christianity worlds apart from modern communism which relies, above everything else, upon the mailed fist of force. Communism doesn't say, "I will give what I have to you." Rather, communism says, "I will take

74

what you have and give it to whomsoever I please."

But there was in the Early Church a communal life which was an expression of the one life that was living in each of those young Christians—a vital, dynamic life. How pale is the modern reproduction of that *Koinonia* fellowship today! As someone said, "We bounce around our fellowship halls like billiard balls ricocheting off the walls when in truth we ought to be crushed together like grapes." How superficial our fellowship often is!

John describes fellowship in his First Epistle. He begins with some hard, cold facts. "That which was from the beginning, which we have heard, which we have seen with our eyes, which we have looked upon, and our hands have handled, of the Word of life; . . . that which we have seen and heard declare we unto you, that ye also may have fellowship with us: and truly our fellowship is with the Father, and with his Son Jesus Christ" (John 1:1,3).

The basis for our fellowship—for this *koinonia*— is the living, risen, resurrected Christ. In effect, John was saying, "We are not fools. This is no cunningly devised fable. This is no mere sentimentality; this is real, hard fact. He is alive! We saw Him. We handled Him. He is alive, and our fellowship with Him is real now and will be forever." It was the word of life eternal that was manifested to these early apostles.

3. How does the apostle John describe "fellowship" in his first epistle? Who is essential to this fellowship? Read again 1 John 1.

John begins first with a fact, and then he proclaims that fact: "That which we have seen and heard declare we unto you" (1 John 1:3). And so it is that if there is to be true fellowship, it must be produced by and based upon a living proclamation, a heralding forth of the glad tidings of the gospel. And so, fellowship springs from evangelism.

But what was John's purpose? He described it when he said, "That ye also may have fellowship with us" (1 John 1:3). People today live in a depersonalized world, alienated even from their neighbors. They live lonelily and without hope, both in this world and in the world to come, when they might enter right now into the most blessed fellowship ever known. For I am confident of one thing: regardless of how anemic is the fellowship we now have, and regardless of how much greater it could be, Christian fellowship is still the greatest fellowship that has ever existed on the face of the earth!

The oneness that Christ Jesus puts into our hearts, the oneness with other fellow believers, is something tremendous to know and to experience. I have found that wherever I go in the world, if I run into a person who has received the living, resurrected Christ, I am his brother and he is mine. This is a thrilling experience. Whether Turk, Arab, Jew, Greek or Roman; if he knows the living Christ, he is my brother, and within minutes we know a rapport that is not found among other people.

Why?

We share the same light from heaven. The same vitalizing principle dwells in us both. We have the same hope, for we worship the same Christ. This fellowship is not only with us, but also "with the Father, and with his Son Jesus Christ" (1 John 1:3).

The Bible says that we can have no fellowship with God without Christ (John 14:20,21,23; 1 John 4:5). The Scriptures declare we cannot have God without having Christ (John 10:30,38; 1 John 2:23). The Bible says we cannot know God without knowing Christ (John 8:19; 14:6-11; 1 John 5:20). We cannot worship God unless we worship Christ (John 5:23; 8:42; 1 John 5:1).

Our fellowship is "with him" (1 John 1:6). This is how we have come to know Him. This is how we have entered into this relationship of *koinonia* with God, where we share in His life and Christ shares His life in us. (See Galatians 2:20.) We have this mutual participation. And what a blessed fellowship it is, this fellowship which having descended vertically from God now moves horizontally among the brethren.

4. What is the scope of Christian fellowship? What do we share in common with all Christians?

John continues in another very important verse by saying, "And these things write we unto you, that your joy may be full" (1 John 1:4). I missed the full meaning of that verse for many years, so I hope that you won't. All those times I had read, "These things write we that your joy may be full."

And what are "these things" that John writes "unto you"? They are that you may know Christ; that you may trust Him; that you may know His love and His light. Yet "these things" are not all that

77

John said. That is just part of it; it is only half the truth.

John also said "unto you" that you might "have fellowship with him" (1 John 1:6). Yes, "unto you" that you "also may have fellowship with us" (1 John 1:3); "unto you" that "your joy may be full" (1 John 1:4).

Those who live a solitary Christian life don't know the fulness of joy that God meant them to know. Those who have never come to the place of really sharing their lives with other Christians and entering into a spiritual fellowship have never known the fulness of joy that God has for them.

Would you have this joy in your life? Then cultivate, seek after, pursue a fellowship of love and sharing—a deep commitment of life one to another.

5. *What very important fact about fellowship had the author missed for so many years? How will you implement this important truth? What will be your reward?*

You should have a Christian friend. Even Christian in *Pilgrim's Progress* had his friend, Faithful. David had his Jonathan; Luther his Melanchthon; Calvin his Beza. They shared their lives together, and thus the fulness of the life of Christ—which is meant to be lived out in a corporate situation—was known.

Do you have a real friend in Christ, a friend with whom you can share? Do you want to see a deepening of that fellowship? Then get down on your knees with that person and share the things of God in prayer. Study the Word of God together with him or her. How long has it been since you were with some friend on your knees together in prayer, confessing your faults, praying for one another, helping one another in the way which leads to life eternal, strengthening one another, and sharing mutual burdens and woes?

If you would do this, you will begin to know something of fellowship that you have never known before. As John said, "That your joy may be full" (1 John 1:4).

But John also describes an essential prerequisite for this fellowship. The Scripture says, "That God is light, and in him is no darkness at all . . . if we walk in the light, as he is in the light, we have fellowship one with another . . ." (1 John 1:5,7).

This is light which reveals, which makes transparent, which makes luminous, clear, plain and readable. Are you walking in the light or are you walking in darkness, covering your life with a veil and hiding your secret sins from God and others? What a wonderful thing it is when you determine to seek after God and walk in His light.

The Bible teaches us to confess our faults one to another and pray for one another. But how little of this is done today. Consequently, people live behind a crusty veneer. They live lonely lives in the midst of crowds. They are unhappy without any deep friendships; no friends with whom they can share their lives. There is always pretense and hypocrisy; a hiding behind the mask. They never really get out into the light and let their lives flow through one another.

The Scripture says, "The blood of Jesus Christ his Son cleanseth us from all sin" (1 John 1:7). How beautiful this is! When we really get honest with one another, we find that our sanctification proceeds; that we are cleansed from sin, not only from its guilt, but also from its power. Of those of us who would pretend we have no sin, John says, "If we say that we have no sin, we deceive ourselves, and the truth is not in us" (1 John 1:8).

6. What is an essential prerequisite for fellowship?

One of the great movements in the Church today is the development of small *koinonia* fellowship groups. These are springing up all over the land where people participate in and share with one another a confluence of heart and life. Often four, six, eight or ten people will come together regularly to read the Bible, pray and share testimonies of strength and victories. They ask one another to pray for them and freely share their failures. They find their lives transformed as they encourage one another and find a strength they never knew before.

7. What has become a great movement in the churches today? What do these groups do?

The Bible says we should provoke one another, in fact, that we should "consider one another to provoke unto love and to good works" (Hebrews 10:24). So I encourage you that if you don't have someone or some group, that you find another

Christian, or several, and really get serious with God. Get honest with God and with one another.

Share this new life that Christ has given you. Dig into a portion of the Bible. Start with the Gospel of John. Read a passage, discuss what it means and pray that God's Spirit will lead you into an understanding of it.

Christ shared His life with us. And He poured it out on a cross. May we share the life He has given us with one another to heal wounded, lonely hearts. Bring the stranger into the fellowship which truly is "with the Father, and with his Son Jesus Christ" (1 John 1:3).

If you have not yet found a church where Jesus Christ is lifted up and honored, where His Word is believed and proclaimed, then I encourage you to find such a church and enter fully into the services and opportunities of worship and study available to you there. God will richly bless you through His Word and the fellowship of other believers in Christ.

8. What must be the essential message of the church we attend? Why?

"Father in Heaven, forgive us because too often we live deceitful lives. We hide our sins, our failings, our weaknesses, lest any should think we are less than perfect. But Thou hast told us we are all sinners, and that, if we say we are not sinners, we are liars. So teach us, Lord, to be honest; to get out of the darkness into the light; to share our lives and enter into that fullness of corporate relationship which Thou meant us to have. May our lives be blessed, enriched and strengthened as we come together in Thee. Help us to grow in Christ and to help others along the way that leads to life eternal. So teach us Lord the secret of *koinonia*. For Christ's sake. Amen."

Study Helps

1. Examine in context the following Bible passages on fellowship: 1 John 1; Colossians 1:18; Hebrews 10:24,25; Acts 2:42,46; Ephesians 4:15,16; 1 John 3:17.

2. Study the *Westminster Confession of Faith*, Chapters 27 and 28: "Of the Church" and "Of the Communion of Saints," in *The Confession of Faith of the Presbyterian Church in the United States*. Richmond, Virginia: The Board of Christian Education, 1965.

3. Read the following books:

Stedman, Ray C. *Body Life*. Glendale, California: Regal Books Division, G/L Publications, 1972.

Graham, Billy. *Peace with God*. New York: Doubleday & Company, Inc., 1953. Note Chapter 15, "The Christian and the Church."

Schaeffer, Francis. *The Mark of the Christian*. Downers Grove, Illinois: Inter-Varsity Press, 1970.

Miller, Keith. *The Taste of New Wine*. Waco, Texas: Word Books, 1965.

Shoemaker, Sam. *Extraordinary Living for Ordinary Men*. Grand Rapids, Michigan: Zondervan Publishing House, 1965. Note Chapter 10, "The Secret of Fellowship."

Gerstner, John H. *Theology for Everyman*. Chicago: Moody Press, 1965. Note chapter on "The Church: Body of Christ."

CHAPTER 6

Transforming the World

I hope your new life with Christ is growing with excitement. In the last chapter we considered the matter of Christian fellowship and the importance of intermingling and sharing your new life with others of like precious faith. I want now to consider the subject of the Church of Christ and its purpose and place in a modern technological society.

This is truly a new and exciting age in which we have been privileged to be born and live. Think how much people in generations past would have given to live in our age and see what we see—men flying to the moon at tremendous speeds. Think what it would have meant to Galileo or da Vinci. But this is our time—a time in the tremendous providence of God that we have been placed on the earth. And it's a wonderful time in which to live in spite of all its problems. It's an age of computers, electronics and data processing. It's a time when the combined knowledge of mankind doubles every ten years.

What about the Church of Jesus Christ in an age

like this? Is this simply some archaic anachronism that doesn't belong in a modern-day world? To many this is just the way it seems. And to many this is just what it has become. To the executive in some great corporation doing tremendous things in this modern world we say, "Come, join the church. It's the greatest thing in the world. We've got some exciting things for you to do. Just think, next Sunday you can take the offering. The following Sunday we're going to let you pass out bulletins. Oh, it's thrilling to be a Christian. The church is such an exciting institution."

No wonder many people today pass the Church by or see it as a sleepy, dead organization, sitting on the corners of most American towns, doing very little of use in an age of tremendous feats and accomplishments. No wonder the younger generation looks at the Church and says, "Man, what's that? Let's go where the action is." This is the image many have of the Church today. No doubt part of the responsibility for this image rests right on the shoulders of the Church because we in the Church have not been what Christ would have us to be. Yet it hasn't always been the way it is today.

What then ought the Church of Jesus Christ to be? Look at it when it was dynamic, fresh-blown from the Master's hand. A handful of men came into a city called Thessalonica, and they hadn't been there but three sabbath days until the whole city was in pandemonium. There was an uproar, the like of which our college activists today wish they were able to bring about. The whole city was turned over. The people gnashed their teeth and cried out, "These that have turned the world upside down are come hither also" (Acts 17:6).

1. What are the characteristics of the Early Church?

The Church isn't being accused of turning the world upside down today, is it? The late Peter Marshall, former chaplain of the United States Senate, used to say that when the early Christians preached there were either riots or regeneration. Today people just yawn, then go home and eat lunch. They say, "That was a nice sermon, Pastor," but they don't really expect anything to be different because of it. Why? Because, I believe, the Church has lost sight of what God meant it to be. J. B. Phillips wrote a book entitled *Your God Is Too Small.* I suppose that if our God is too small, then His Church —that is, our vision of His Church—is also too small.

I wonder how many of us believe that the most important thing happening in the world today is happening in the Church of Jesus Christ? It is more important than space travel, visits to Mars or the Vietnam war. It is more important than business, technology or developments in economics. Yes, it is more important than anything else. I doubt there are many people today who see the Church in this light.

2. What are the characteristics of the Church today? What is the church like in which you worship?

Consider with me exactly what the Church is like. The Church of Jesus Christ is center stage in this world. Everything else that happens is just the backdrop, the scenery, for the real action—the eternal transformation of human beings. We need to hear again the voice of Jesus Christ as He speaks to His people. We need to hear clearly the message that He brings. The message that He gave to His Church when He called His people unto Himself (Matthew 10; Mark 3:13-15; 6:7-13; Luke 9:1-6; 10:1-24) was, in effect, simply this: "Come, help transform the world." And this is my challenge to you now, "Come, help transform the world."

The way the world will be changed, according to Christ, is not via the method of the social gospel, that is, by reorganizing the external affairs of men. The world is going to be permanently changed only when the hearts of men and women are changed by God. You can take the same sinful people, shuffle them around, restack them one way or another, reorganize and redistribute them, but they are still going to be the same immoral, covetous, greedy, selfish, proud, hateful, miserable individuals they were before, unless Christ changes their hearts.

Jesus did not preach slum clearance. He did not take men out of the slums. He took the slums out of men, and soon men got rid of the slums. Because you see, as a man "thinketh in his heart, so is he" (Proverbs 23:7). The world is what it is because of what individual human beings are in their hearts.

3. *What command did Jesus Christ give to His Church? How is this to be realized?*

Recently on television there was a program about the medical ship *Hope*, a tremendous venture of compassion. The program showed the many countries to which the ship had gone. It also showed the extreme poverty, disease and ignorance that plagued these nations. I thought to myself, "Why is it that there are some nations that receive the good ship *Hope* into their hopelessness, and other nations that send ships of hope?" Have you considered that? It is not by accident, nor is it a freak of fate. It can be carefully, historically analyzed. The ultimate reason is religion.

Why?

Because people are what they believe and think in their hearts. It is a fact that men are what they are because of what they believe. As a man "thinketh in his heart, so is he," the Bible says (Proverbs 23:7). And Christ said almost the same thing when He declared, "A good man out of the good treasure of the heart bringeth forth good things: and an evil man out of the evil treasure bringeth forth evil things" (Matthew 12:35).

Yes, this is what Christ has taught us, and this is what history has confirmed over and over again, and upon which it has placed its imprimatur. It is incontrovertible.

4. What is always the basis of any man's thinking? What is the basis of your thinking?

Why is it that some nations languish in their squalor? It is because of what they believe. It is because of their god. It is the fatalism of the Muslim world that has strangled their initiative and kept them in the bondage of their sin, depravity, ignorance and squalor. It is the pantheism of Hinduism which has blotted out the distinction between right and wrong, morality and immorality, and has kept the great masses of India in the condition they find themselves today. It is the pure pagan superstition of China that through thousands of years has kept these people on a subsistence level. It is the superstition of the Christian-pagan Romanism of South America that has kept the continent in the condition it is while North America has progressed as no other part of the world has. Men are what they are because of what they believe.

It is the gospel of Jesus Christ that has set men free, that has severed the bonds that held them in captivity. It is the gospel of Jesus Christ which has produced literacy in the world. All you have to do to confirm this is to check the statistics, and you will see that this is so. The nations where the true gospel of Christ has gone are the nations that have learned to read, and with that have come all of the blessings of civilization. In other places where the gospel has been chained, people languish in their ignorance.

Oh, that God would take away the blinders from our eyes so that we might see the important role Christians play in the world. "Ye are the salt of the earth. . . . Ye are the light of the world," said Christ (Matthew 5:13,14). And this is the only thing which prevents complete corruption, decay and putrefaction of this world.

5. What has been the worldwide effect of the gospel (or good news) of Jesus Christ?

If the gospel of Christ is so important, and if the Church of Christ is center stage in the great drama of this world, then a strategy is needed for the propagation of this life-changing message to an expanding world population. The dictionary defines strategy as "the employment of resources to achieve a definite objective." The main problem is that the Church has lost sight of its objective. The reason the Church is not doing what it ought to do is that it doesn't even know what it ought to be doing. It just keeps going through the motions, just keeping the wheels going. People talk to me about such-and-such a church and say that church needs them. I have asked them "For what?" People have lost sight of what the Church is in the world to do.

6. Why is the Church not doing what it has been commanded to do by Jesus Christ?

What is your life objective now that you are a Christian? Having come into the family of God, Christ has given you an objective which is the objective of every single redeemed member of that family. And that objective, simply stated is this, "Go ye into all the world, and preach the gospel to every creature" (Mark 16:15). This is the Great Commission which has been given to the Church by its King, its Lord, its General. This is our task in life. Nothing else will suffice. No amendments may be offered to the motion. It is not debatable. It cannot be countermanded, for it is the command of a King. It is the marching orders of the General. It is the chief object or goal of His Church. It is the command of God for your life and for mine. "Go ye into all the world, and preach the gospel to every creature" (Mark 16:15).

7. What is the life objective for every believer?

You may say, "It's too big, I can't get my mind around it." Every businessman knows it is not enough just to have a definite objective and to spell it out clearly. You must also have, in addition to the long-range objective, a step-by-step procedure which will enable you to reach that goal. There must be an intermediate goal; there must be short range goals; and there must be immediate actions taken. What are these and how are they to be done?

Strategy is the employment of resources to reach a definite objective. We have seen what the objective is; namely, the evangelization of the world in this generation. This can be done in this generation as never before in history. Someone has alleged, "If every professing Christian were to tell the gospel to someone else and lead them to Christ today, and all of those were to do the same tomorrow, we would have to quit before suppertime because there would not be enough people to win."

Does that sound strange?

Well, there are over nine hundred million professing Christians in the world, the largest institution that has ever existed. There are 3.5 billion people in the world. Simple arithmetic will show us that you can't double nine hundred million today and then double it again tomorrow because that would be almost four billion people. Therefore, the evangelization of the world could be accomplished in two days if every Christian were simply to do his job.

What then are our resources? I am reminded of a story I once heard about a man who lived in the thirties in west Texas. He had a farm which he had worked for years, and things had gone from bad to worse. Rain was scant, there wasn't much food, and he was about to lose his farm. He was desperate. About that time, some oil men came to him and said, "From our reports we think there is oil on your property and we would like to drill."

They signed a contract and sank a well.

At eleven hundred feet they hit a pool of oil. Only it wasn't a pool; it was an ocean of oil. It was the largest find ever discovered. They pumped out 80,000 barrels a day. That's a quarter of a million dollars a day. Then they sank another well, and that one came in at 180,000 barrels a day; and then another, and another, and another, and still they are going at an average of 125,000 barrels to this day. For years that man had lived in poverty, yet all that time he had been a millionaire, a billionaire, even a multi-billionaire, and hadn't known it. Though wealthy beyond his wildest dreams, he had been unable to pay the mortgage on his farm or even feed his family.

What a picture this is of the Church today! Yet "Jesus came and spake unto them, saying, All power is given unto me in heaven and in earth. . . . Go ye into all the world, and preach the gospel to every creature. . . . Ye shall receive power, after that the Holy Ghost is come upon you: and ye shall be witnesses unto me . . ." (Matthew 28:18; Mark 16:15; Acts 1:8). There is the power of God. "Call unto me, and I will answer thee, and shew thee great and mighty things, which thou knowest not" (Jeremiah 33:3). Oh, that many would come to call in faith upon that great God of ours, reaching out, drilling down and taking hold of the resources of God. These are the divine resources.

8. *What resources does God make available to us for worldwide proclamation of the gospel?*

But there is a human resource as well. There is a divine key which God has given for this great task to which we have been commissioned. Christ showed us the way He was going to reach the world. Jesus never traveled to Athens, never preached at the Parthenon, never went to Corinth or Rome. Rather, Jesus invested His life in a small group of people. He trained them thoroughly, and He trained them to train others.

This was His key: the spiritual multiplication of the Church. This is the key we need to regrasp today. This is our churches all over the world and to make pastors realize it is only through the training and equipping of the laity that the job of world evangelism can be done.

9. *What method has God ordained or instituted for worldwide proclamation of the gospel?*

93

God has singularly designed it so that you are one of those who can most effectively perform the Great Commission that He has given to us all. You rub shoulders every day with the masses of this world, so you have the opportunity of reaching thousands of people.

God has given pastors and teachers to the Church in order that we might equip the saints to do the work of ministering. According to the New Testament, every Christian is a saint (Ephesians 2:19), a sanctified one (1 Corinthians 1:2), a separated one (Romans 7:1), a cleansed one (Ephesians 5:26,27). And every Christian is a minister with a ministry to perform (2 Corinthians 5:17—6:10). You as a Christian, yes as a lay Christian, have a ministry to which God has called you. And it is the ministry of the clergyman to equip you to perform more effectively the ministry that God has given to you. However, instead of fulfilling this task as Christ has commanded us to do it—through the laity—we pastors try too often to do it all ourselves. Meanwhile, our congregations sit as spectators watching the pastors work, patting us on the back and saying, "Good job, preacher." Therefore, our immediate goal is to reach pastors and train them to equip their people for the opportunities which are theirs.

10. Why is the local pastor so important in reaching the whole world for Christ?

Can this be done? Yes it can. In the past few years, I've spoken to over 25,000 ministers myself on this very subject. We know that all over our country and all over the world, there is a great spiritual awakening taking place. Ten years ago this would have been utterly incredible. Even five years ago there was little sign of such an awakening. But today ministers everywhere are catching the vision, and now churches are beginning to see the need for and the importance of training and equipping laymen in small groups and private Bible studies for evangelism. Also, lay Christians themselves are realizing that evangelism is both their privilege and their responsibility.

One of the most basic needs of the human heart is the need for adventure, God made us to be great adventurers for Him. This need for adventure is what took Columbus across the ocean. This is what takes men to the moon and will take them to the stars. But the greatest adventure in all the world is to be a co-laborer with God and take men to heaven. Do you see why the Church of Jesus Christ is the greatest adventure in the world?

11. Why is the Church of Jesus Christ the greatest adventure in the world?

Now let us consider for a moment our short-range goal. How are we to do this? One way is by setting an example. This begins right here at home. What are we doing right here as a local church? And what are you doing as a part of that church to make it what it ought to be? By the power of God's Spirit, what can the Church be? It will come to pass that the Church will be what it ought to be when men and women are committed totally to Christ, saying, "Lord, here is my heart, my mind, my talent, my intellect, my body, my hands, my mouth and my feet. Take them and use them for Thee, Lord. I want to get into the army, into the battle. I'm tired of sitting on the sidelines, of being AWOL. I want to fight the good fight of faith. I want to be used to spread the glad tidings of eternal life, the gift of God."

Some will say, "In the early days of the Christian Church, the world hadn't heard of Christ. The Resurrection was something new and exciting, but today it's old hat." But if this were true, why is it that most of our people today are in utter and complete spiritual darkness? They haven't the faintest idea of what the gospel of Christ is. Seventy-five percent of them suppose eternal life is something you have to earn or deserve, or merit. They've never heard it is a free gift. It is as great news today as it ever was to tell people that by simple trust in the cross of Christ, they may receive the forgiveness of their sins and the gift of eternal life; that they can be completely transformed and can know they are going to heaven. These glad tidings are as joyous today as when the angels first sang them on that Christmas night so long ago!

12. What is the gospel of Jesus Christ, and why is it just as good news today as it was in the first century?

But how are others going to hear? This is up to you. What the Church needs today is not just a few hundred, but thousands and millions of involved people telling the gospel of Christ to others. What we need everywhere are congregations where everyone is saying, "Lord, you've said that I'm to be a witness for You, and by Your grace that's what I'm going to be."

This was the secret power of the Early Church. We read all "they that were scattered abroad went every where preaching the word" (Acts 8:4). And the term used in the Greek text for "preaching" means "evangelizing," proclaiming the evangel, the tidings of the gospel of the free grace of God. Somebody might say, "Doesn't that refer only to the apostles?" Well, let's look at the context here since a text without a context is a pretext.

We read in the eighth chapter of Acts and verse one, that "they were all scattered abroad . . . except the apostles." And those "that were scattered abroad went every where preaching the word" (Acts 8:4), sharing the good news with others.

This is how the whole world was turned upside down. This is how it happened that the greatest, most powerful pagan empire this world has ever seen was overthrown by the power of the Word of Christ. It was done by thousands and millions of simple, everyday Christians witnessing to the power of the gospel of Christ. Christians sharing with others, unashamed and unafraid, willing to identify themselves with Jesus Christ and not fearful of being called fanatics.

There is the only thing in this world worth getting fanatical about. Did you ever stop to think about the men who stand up, shout, scream, wave their arms, jump up and down and make absolute idiots of themselves at a football game? We call them "fans." But if a person gets the least bit enthusiastic about Jesus Christ who rose from the dead and offers us eternal life, that person is called a "fanatic." Let them say what they will. The problem is they are demonstrating that they are blind, deaf, and dead in their sins. One day they will stand before the great judgment seat of God—that great white throne—and there they will see that they were the fools.

As I have already said, we must have short-range goals. We must learn to share the gospel of Christ. We must learn to lay hold of the throne of God in prayer, see His power and be filled with the Spirit of God. We must also be sure we are God's men and God's women doing His work anywhere and everywhere. We must learn how to take advantage of the thousands of opportunities to witness that are ours every week.

A businessman recently brought the gospel to several hundred life insurance underwriters in this city. Not too long ago a lady spoke to the Junior Women's Club and made a magnificent presentation of the gospel of Jesus Christ. She challenged and grasped the hearts of those who heard her. Another Christian man went to an avante-garde art group and presented the gospel of Christ. Some of the leading people in town were challenged.

Some businessmen used their own money to invite all of the leaders of a high school to a banquet and there an outstanding speaker presented the gospel to the leading athletes, cheerleaders and intellectuals of the school. The young people were absolutely silent as many of them, for the first time, heard the claims of Jesus Christ, of Him who died and rose again that they might have life eternal. They went out of that place, and scores of these young leaders committed their lives to Christ. Why? Because some laymen cared enough about them to do something about it.

In whatever capacity you find yourself there are many opportunities for witness. If your church is like most churches today, they are providing opportunities for learning how to share your faith in Christ. I hope that after having received the greatest Gift in the world you will want to pass it on. One young lady said to me recently, "Don't simply keep the faith, pass it on." I hope you will speak to the one that spoke to you about Christ and ask how you might learn to share your faith more effectively with others so that you can become a part of what truly is the greatest adventure in the world.

Jesus said, "Go ye into all the world, and preach the gospel to every creature" (Mark 16:15). Share the glad tidings of eternal life. Unfortunately, most church members haven't even bothered to go next door. Jesus said, "Go," and we sit. He said, "Go," and we wait while all around us is a world that is perishing and slipping away into everlasting darkness without the knowledge of the Saviour. God can use your life to bring eternal life to some of these dying men and women.

13. *What is the challenge placed before you? What will you do about it? Who will train you to share your faith effectively with others?*

There is an incident that happened some years ago at a lifeguard station in New England. It had been built there because nearby were dangerous rocks and reefs, where ships frequently crashed and sank. One night a hurricane wracked that New England Coast with roaring winds and mountainous waves. A large ship was being blown closer and closer to the dangerous reefs as jagged rocks reached out to tear the ship apart.

An alarm was sounded as a radio message for help came into that lifeguard station. The captain pulled a switch, and bells rang and sirens howled as men leaped from their beds and fell in. They were all well-trained men and ready to go.

"Man the boats!" the captain shouted.

But a boatswain came to him and said, "Sir, have you seen those waves out there? They're the size of mountains. We'll never make it out to that ship."

"Man the boats," the captain repeated.

The boatswain saluted and went out. But a few minutes later he came back and said, "Sir, it's no use. Even if we could possibly get out through those waves to the ship, we would never get back alive again."

The captain looked the man straight in the eyes and sternly replied, "Boatswain, we *must* go out! We don't have to come back!"

"Oh, God our Father, forgive us that we have lost sight of our goal which You have given to Your church. Forgive us even more that we have lost the heart for the fight; that too often we have been ashamed of Jesus and our lips have been silent while the world goes to hell. We have deserted our posts and the ships have sunk.

"Oh, God, may Thy Spirit in a supernatural way move upon our hearts this day so that we can do nothing else but obey Thy voice who didst say, 'Go, go into a lost world and proclaim the glad tidings of eternal life.' Oh, Thou who didst say, 'Call unto Me,' we call and ask that Thou wouldst help us in the name of Jesus Christ, the King of kings to transform our world. Amen."

Study Helps

1. Examine in their context the following Bible passages on witness: Matthew 28:18-20; Mark 16:14-16; Luke 24:44-49; Acts 1:8; 4:12; 8:1-4; Romans 10:8-15; Mark 10:32,33.

2. Study the *Westminster Confession of Faith,* Chapter 10: "Of the Gospel," in *The Confession of Faith of the Presbyterian Church in the United States.* Richmond, Virginia: The Board of Christian Education, 1965.

3. Read the following books:

Stott, John. *Our Guilty Silence.* Grand Rapids, Michigan: William B. Eerdmans Publishing Company, 1969.

Chandler, E. Russell. *The Kennedy Explosion.* Elgin, Illinois: David C. Cook Publishing Co., 1971.

Little, Paul E. *How to Give Away Your Faith.* Downers Grove, Illinois: Inter-Varsity Press, 1970.

Packer, J.I. *Evangelism and the Sovereignty of God.* Downers Grove, Illinois: Inter-Varsity Press, 1970.

Ford, Leighton. *The Christian Persuader*. New York: Harper & Row, Publishers, 1966.

Kennedy, D. James. *Evangelism Explosion*. Wheaton, Illinois: Tyndale House, Publishers, 1971.

Bright, Bill. *Revolution Now!* San Bernardino: Campus Crusade for Christ, Inc., 1969.

Chantry, Walter. *Today's Gospel*. Swengel, Pennsylvania: Reiner Publications, 1970.

Trotman, Dawson. *Born to Reproduce*. Colorado Springs: The Navigators, n.d.

Ridenour, Fritz. *Tell It Like It Is*. Glendale, California: Regal Books Division, G/L Publications, 1968.